If both people in a couple come from supportive, nurturing families, they will bring few wounds and deficits into their adult relationships. It will be quite normal for them to expect from each other such things as love, support, involvement, protection, and sharing of material items.

However, if either (or both) enters a relationship wounded or with a serious lack from childhood, the need and longing for what is missing will be intense. Such couples knowingly or unknowingly make contracts with each other to make up for what they lacked as children.

There are several types of contracts (agreements) that these couples design. The danger is that the contract may not be spoken. And because it is never actually put into words, there is no conscious and open agreement between the two people. An unspoken contract is like a minefield ready to explode without warning. If one woman in a relationship believes there is an important unspoken agreement that has been broken, the results can be disastrous.

If a woman is *unaware* of what she wants from her partner, desires of which she is unconscious will become the basis of an unspoken contract. If a woman is *aware* of what she wants from her partner but neglects to say it or is unwilling to say it, her withheld desires also become the basis of an unspoken contract.

Women who are aware of what they need and are willing to state their needs form spoken contracts, the advantage being that both partners clearly understand the agreement.

THE
LOVING
LESBIAN

BY
Claire McNab
AND
Sharon Gedan

THE NAIAD PRESS, INC.
1997

Printed in the United States of America on acid-free paper
First Edition

Editor: Lila Empson
Cover designer: Bonnie Liss (Phoenix Graphics)
Typesetter: Sandi Stancil

Library of Congress Cataloging-in-Publication Data

McNab, Claire.
    The loving lesbian / Claire McNab and Sharon Gedan.
        p.   cm.
    ISBN 1-56280-169-4 (alk. paper)
    1. Lesbianism. 2. Lesbians—Psychology. 3. Love. I. Gedan,
Sharon, 1943 – . II. Title.
HQ75.5.M45   1997
306.76′63—dc21   96-45485
                                                                              CIP

To Kayla   (S. G.)

To Sheila   (C. McN.)

Acknowledgments

The authors wish to thank Lila Empson and Sandi Stancil for editing and typesetting, respectively. Where would we be without their superior skills?

About the Authors

Los Angeles–based psychotherapist Sharon Gedan has devoted her 28-year career to helping lesbian and gay individuals and couples develop satisfying and dynamic relationships. She has lectured, given workshops, and made media appearances across the country.

Although Claire McNab is best known for her mystery series featuring Detective Inspector Carol Ashton, the most recent being *Inner Circle,* she spent many years in her native Australia teaching psychology and communications courses.

Contents

AUTHOR'S NOTE: The case studies in *The Loving Lesbian* do not name actual women or detail the events of their lives. Rather, the case studies are imaginary composites of all the lessons I have learned from my clients throughout the many years of my practice.   —S. G.

Foreword

Lesbians are in the process of moving beyond the dictates of history. Lesbian relationships demonstrate that societal constraints have less power than they once did. This book reflects what is best in lesbian relationships and provides practical guidance to enhance the work women do to develop and enjoy their relationships.

Lesbians, like all women, to some extent have internalized society's messages about women's worth and roles in life, and they bring these concepts to their relationships. *The Loving Lesbian* assists women to increase their awareness of what has been in-

ternalized, so that they become more able to reach
out to each other with generosity and love.

The Loving Lesbian celebrates the work done by
so many women to discern what is true in their feelings and ways of relating and celebrates their efforts
to let go of false identities taken on to adapt to
societal pressures.

Women are naturally gifted in the art of relating,
yet such talents flourish or wither depending on the
care and attention that is given to their development.
Loving relationships are experienced by women who
accept each other on a real basis and who encourage
each other to be whole. These relationships may last
a month, a year, or a lifetime. It is the respect for
oneself and for the other person that distinguishes
them.

Some women seem to be naturally better at being
loving. Usually these women were mentored by
parents or caretakers who themselves had learned to
be loving and therefore demonstrated loving behaviors. All women can learn to express themselves
more lovingly, whether building on a solid foundation
from childhood or learning for the first time as
adults.

A commitment to a loving relationship is a commitment to self-awareness, self-development, and
sharing of self. This book is written for women who
welcome the challenges, the delights, and the
long-term rewards of loving.

Lesbian communities are affected by the quality
and stability of the relationships within them. As
with any minority group, lesbian communities are
weakened as much by internal struggles as they are
by external attacks. The strength of individual

relationships — at the level of friends and of sexual partners — provides the basis for the energy and vigor of the community.

The Loving Lesbian explores the unique qualities and potentials of lesbian love — the problems, the challenges, the rich rewards.

The central aim of this book is to strengthen the commitment women have to each other and to support experiences and attitudes that welcome and nourish love.

Introduction

Now that I am in the middle of my life, I believe it is love that infuses life with meaning, not just the delicious feeling of the emotion, but the ongoing discovery of whether my love can make a successful journey from my heart into the everyday exchanges of life. Loving is simple. The challenge is clearing a path for its honest expression.

Growing up on the south side of Chicago in the fifties, I had little consciousness of love and loving. The rigors of daily life in our working class, multiracial, multiethnic neighborhood preempted expressions of love. My mother's energies shifted from home to hard work after my father was diagnosed with a devastating psychiatric illness.

We made weekly trips to the state psychiatric facility that housed my father. It was a two-hour trek by bus and elevated train in a vain search for a family feeling, which could not be experienced in such a desolate place.

My life shifted from concerns about survival and safety when a scholarship to a college in California offered the opportunity for a rich education and a protective environment in which to explore ideas. This began my examination of the psychology of love. My friendship with my college roommate, Marianne Stanley Boretz, now Ph.D., for the first time gave me the opportunity to share, intellectually and emotionally, my inner world. I now see this sharing as the basis and the essence of intimate love.

I continue to learn about what love is, and what it is not, each day from the family, friends, and animals who are my companions on this interesting journey. Thanks to my dear friend, Linus Pauling Jr., M.D., who is a loving guide, to my aunt Rose Groenandal, who demonstrates that loving God and living fully are compatible, and to my partner, Kayla Pressman, who teaches me that loyalty, laughter, and friendship provide good housing for love.

This book is primarily based on what I have learned from my twenty-eight-year experience as a therapist participating in my clients' struggles to achieve love of self and loving relationships. Thank you to each of you who have invited me into your private world, where we have confronted together the pain that makes love feel risky and have removed the disguises that pain has employed to make us think that loving is unwise or unnecessary.

In addition to the insights I have gained through personal experience, I have included the wisdom of some of the many writers and researchers who have enriched my work.

My thanks to Elizabeth Nonas and Nancy Bereano for their help in gathering resources for this book.

— Sharon Gedan

Chapter 1:
Lesbian Love Is Unique

The depth of emotion between women distinguishes
lesbian relationships from all others.

Women usually have access to their feelings and
an interest in sharing their emotional experiences.
This sharing creates a sense of intimacy and excitement.

Two women are capable of a sexual exchange that
can be tender and exquisite, passionate, a true
merging — which at times creates a spiritual level of
sexuality as well as one of high passion and pleasure.

Why is this?

First, each woman has experiences with her own

body's responses, so there is a matching responsiveness and understanding of a partner's body.

Second, women value closeness, warmth, and communication during sexual exchange, and those shared feelings create a compelling desire to relate and to make emotional contact.

Understanding each other's bodies so intimately, two women have an innate sense of the tempo and flow of building excitement to the point of climax. There is an acceptance and awareness that allows each woman to proceed at her own pace. Lesbians often will say how much they enjoy a slow process — the stroking, touching, talking, holding, and hugging. Others report an intensity of passion that comes from a partner's intuitive and immediate responses to the movements and changes in their bodies and feelings — "It was like she was inside of all of me."

Feelings of being one are created by sharing, by noticing and focusing on similarities, and by flowing sexual experiences. The warmth and sensuality of a female body invites touch. The doubled sweetness of two women creates both a craving for, and the possibility of, deep sexual satisfaction.

Some unique aspects of lesbian love create challenges. The closeness between lesbians can lead to a merging in which one or both women feel they are losing a sense of who they are as separate independent beings. They may begin to look or sound like each other and may give up separate interests or friends.

Society also contributes to the challenges lesbians face. Close relationships between women are generally accepted, and most women have at least one intimate female friend. Lesbians do experience discrimination, which may be subtle or direct to the point of violence, but society does not feel as threatened as by gay men, and lesbians are therefore not subjected to the same level of hatred and physical violence.

Because society is accustomed to women relating closely, lesbian couples may not be recognized as such. While this creates some safety from discrimination, there is a downside to this comparative invisibility. Lesbian relationships are often not acknowledged as real couplings and, although two lesbians may refer to themselves as *we* and may appear together at family and public functions, it is common for them to hear comments about meeting a nice man or queries about "settling down."

In reality, up to 10 percent of all women are lesbians. With or without support from their families and peers, lesbians form relationships, raise families, work, and contribute to the general community. There is a justified sense of pride in the success of lesbian relationships and community organizations against the societal odds.

Beginning in the nineties, lesbian characters began appearing regularly in movies and television series. While those characters do not yet present a complete picture of the range of lesbian lifestyles, the mass culture's consciousness about lesbians is being reshaped as people see lesbians portrayed in ordinary life situations.

The Lesbian Family

Lesbian weddings appear on prime-time television. "Lesbian Baby Boom" is featured on the cover of

Harper's Bazaar. Legislation that would grant lesbians the legal status conferred by marriage is being argued in state legislatures and courts. While it may take many years to resolve the question of marriage, lesbian couples and lesbian family issues have become visible because of the wide media coverage given to such issues.

Lesbian families are diverse: couples; couples with children; singles with children; singles or couples with live-in parents or other relatives; three or more singles forming a family unit; singles or couples with an acquired family of close, sometimes lifelong, friends; singles or couples with grandchildren, god-children, nieces and nephews and family pets. Fathers of the children of lesbian mothers are sometimes an integral part of the family life and may even have part-time custody.

Among lesbians age forty and under, there is often a sense of entitlement about family life that did not previously exist. The risks taken and accomplishments achieved by lesbians during the seventies and eighties have resulted in the expectation that single lesbians and lesbian couples have the right and the freedom to select any option available in family and community life.

Lesbian families face special challenges. These include the acquisition of adequate income; availability of safe, acceptable sperm; decisions whether one or both women will bear children; determination of the role the father will play, if any; successful adoption; and concern about society's acceptance of children who come from lesbian families.

Support groups for lesbians working with fertility issues, children of lesbians, and couples counseling can be found in many gay and lesbian churches, synagogues, and community centers.

Francesca, 36, and Melanie, 42, have been together for five years. They share a comfortable two-bedroom apartment and have often referred to the second bedroom as the baby's room. Both women want children. Francesca is unable to overcome her fears of getting AIDS through a sperm bank or of getting sperm from a donor with some undetected genetic flaw. Melanie feels she is getting too old to give birth, but worries that an adopted child would be more likely to have problems than a child one of them might have. Francesca or Melanie feel that there is no one whom they could approach personally for sperm.

This couple, unable to resolve their personal issues about having children, decided to become involved with Melanie's sister's son and daughter. As active aunts, they can satisfy some of their needs to nurture. They also volunteer at the local grammar school, tutoring children learning to read.

Allison and Dana are a two-career couple. Allison is the chief financial officer for a medium-size business and Dana is a paramedic. Dana never considered having children, although she enjoys her nieces and nephews. Allison has wanted a child since she was in high school. Now at 32 and in a relationship for four years, she feels ready.

Dana and Allison have good communication skills and have discussed the idea of having a child for some time. Dana realizes that she is afraid of the commitment involved. Although she loves Allison, she is keenly aware that if trouble arose in their relationship, it would be easier for her to leave if there was no baby involved.

Although she wants a baby, Allison decides that she will not break up the relationship over this issue.

Dana realizes how committed Allison is to her, and that she had originally felt threatened at the thought of sharing Allison with a baby.

As they continue to talk through the issue, both women feel that they better understand each other's feelings and needs. They decide that they will raise a child together and approach Dana's cousin for sperm. After three months of trying, Allison becomes pregnant.

Jackie is a house painter and Beth is in her junior year of college. Both are 20 and have been seeing each other for a year. Beth and Jackie are very much in love, and Beth would like to have a baby as soon as possible. "My mother had me when she was nineteen. I don't want to wait much longer."

Jackie and Beth's families accept their relationship, and everyone openly discusses the economic realities of living together and raising a family. With guidance from each family, Jackie and Beth decide that they will not live together until Beth finishes college. In the meantime, Jackie will take classes to obtain a contractor's license and raise her income, and Beth will get a teaching credential so she can contribute financially and have a work schedule that is compatible with raising children.

These three couples represent a few of the many

options women select in shaping their family structures.

Adoption

One of the options lesbian couples are more frequently considering is adoption.

Jane Haven, Ph.D., Los Angeles psychologist specializing in adoption, urges women to seek out the highest quality adoption professionals (a) who are in good standing with their state bar or licensing boards and (b) who can provide references from lesbian couples with whom they have worked in the past. Because most states do not allow open adoption to lesbian couples, expert advice can help women with successful adoption strategies.

Whatever form the lesbian family takes, a loving atmosphere is created and maintained by:

- Communicating frankly and sensitively with family members
- Agreeing on the goals of the family
- Dealing with discrimination
- Maintaining adequate support for the family in both practical and emotional areas

Woman + woman creates a relationship that has the potential for unique closeness and understanding.

Women relate significantly on emotional and sexual levels, so each woman can respond to the other with an intense, comforting warmth.

Chapter 2:

Reasons for Relationships

Many people, including lesbians, believe that love in some way will transform their lives, filling in the empty spaces and making everything worthwhile.

What Love Can and Cannot Do

While it is true that love brings joy and meaning to life, it is important to understand some common beliefs about what love can and cannot do.

Love will make up for lacks in childhood. Many people come into adulthood feeling eager to relate and believing they are ready for love. However, if they have serious deficits from childhood — the four most common are lack of love, nurturing, good parenting, and approval — they are *not* ready for love. They are ready to complete the process of growing up. When such a woman forms a close lesbian relationship, her childhood deficits become obvious and place great strain on the partnership. If, at some level, she feels that she doesn't really deserve to be loved, it's possible that she may unconsciously sabotage relationship after relationship.

Love will transform life. This statement is both true and false. The false aspect is related to the fact that a woman first has to *have* a life, in order to share it with someone else. No single intimate relationship can possibly fulfill every need. Each woman needs to have other relationships, which can include family, either blood or acquired, and a support system of friends, as well as things that give her life a sense of purpose and fullness, such as work, spirituality, hobbies, interests, children.

The true aspect of the statement comes into operation when a woman *does* bring a full life to a relationship. Then she and her partner will find that love does transform, making their lives richer and more rewarding.

Relationships: Why and Why Not

Why women start a relationship:

• To satisfy a sexual attraction
• To avoid being alone
• To enjoy the first phase of a relationship

- To be loved
- To love someone
- To have a committed relationship

Why women DON'T start a relationship:

- Fear of rejection
- Fear of closeness
- Lack of self-confidence
- She is basically a loner
- Failure to find a compatible person who attracts her
- Problems with drugs and alcohol
- Emotional problems

Why women commit to a relationship:

- To share love and affection
- To have a consistent sexual partner
- To have companionship
- To share daily tasks
- To share expenses
- To raise children
- Because of social pressures to be in a relationship
- To create a richer personal and social life

Why women DON'T commit to a relationship:

- Fear of loss of freedom, fear of rejection, or fear that the relationship will end
- Time and experience with each other reveals incompatibilities

- The person doesn't believe in commitment for personal or political reasons
- A compelling and unexpected change in the couple's life, such as transfer to another location, illness of a parent, diagnosis of a serious illness, eruption of an emotional problem
- Problems with commitment
- Self-centeredness
- Immaturity

What Have I Got to Offer to a Relationship?

Use the following checklist to become aware of what you have to offer in a relationship. Each statement lists something people look for in a partner.

Personal Attributes Checklist

	YES	NO
1. I have a good sense of humor.	☐	☐
2. I'm willing to talk when there's a problem.	☐	☐
3. I enjoy sex.	☐	☐
4. I'm a good friend.	☐	☐
5. I'm a good listener.	☐	☐
6. I can support myself financially.	☐	☐
7. I'm fun to be with.	☐	☐
8. I enjoy my work/school.	☐	☐
9. I have leisure time activities I enjoy.	☐	☐
10. I take care of my appearance.	☐	☐
11. I take care of my health.	☐	☐
12. I have useful skills.	☐	☐
13. I'm intelligent.	☐	☐

14. I'm attractive.   □   □
15. I'm a loving person.   □   □
16. I have friends.   □   □
17. I know how to be emotionally supportive.   □   □
18. I'm willing to try new things.   □   □
19. I'm honest.   □   □

Were you aware of these qualities in yourself before you did the above checklist? If not, you need to pay more attention to the positive things about yourself. If you approach someone with a positive self-awareness, you present yourself more favorably and more confidently and are therefore more likely to attract the person in whom you're interested.

Relationships Enrich Both Women's Lives

Tina and Marty met on a women's softball league the summer after high school. They played against each other and had a shouting match after the final call in a 3–2 championship game.

There has been more shouting in their thirty-year relationship, but both of them tear up when they talk about enriching each other's lives.

"Tina's family has taken me in. I couldn't imagine a holiday or something special in my life without them. My parents died when I was young, and my brother was killed in 'Nam. She gave me a family — with eight sisters-and-brothers-in-law!"

"I never would have had a kid or gotten a real estate license if Marty hadn't believed in me — and us. She overcame so much in her own life that she inspired me. I taught her to cook Italian and she introduced me to reading everything from classics to sci-fi."

Lesbian relationships offer women exposure to the talents, interests, and people in their partners' lives. Also, it is often easier for each woman to have the individual experiences that enrich her life when she feels emotionally secure and supported by her partner.

You'd Love a Long-Term Relationship, But . . .

If you have experienced multiple short-term relationships and want to have a long-term relationship — *want* to, not just think you should — consider the following possibilities.

1. You are looking for the perfect partner. Some people imagine that when they find that perfect partner a wonderful relationship will automatically develop. You are guarding your heart and withholding commitment from possible partners who are compatible and worthwhile while you search for perfection.

The fact that you have to work at developing and maintaining a relationship is not a sign that you've picked the wrong person. It is simply the nature of relationships.

2. You withhold yourself from commitments of all kinds. You see commitments as cages that will confine and limit you. It's important for you to develop a more balanced view of commitment, which includes both a sense of responsibility to a partner and the ability to remain a separate person.

3. You are uncomfortable when people get too close to you. Individuals need and enjoy varying degrees of togetherness. Avoid labeling your own closeness comfort zone a problem. You are you, and there is no point in comparing your needs for space to other people. This is an issue that should be discussed with the woman you are seeing to establish how much closeness each of you enjoys, and how much distance and privacy each of you needs.

If you have become less comfortable with closeness after experiencing traumatic events such as painful breakups, betrayals, deaths, you may need to talk with a therapist or a spiritual counselor so that you can learn to trust again.

4. You don't want to deal with everything you see coupled friends going through. No one does. You might want to ask your friends why it is worth it to them. Many couples report that closeness, security, fun, and opportunity for personal growth make it worthwhile.

5. You have experienced loss in your past and don't want to expose yourself to the possibility of that pain again. You may or may not be conscious of how much past loss influences your present behavior.

Sandra is 34 and has started relationships with twenty women since she came out at age 19. She is warm and lively and easily attracts women. With six of the women she felt interested enough to consider making a commitment, and with two she felt sure that she had found her permanent partner. But each time, after six months to a year, she found herself pulling away. Sandra could usually find reasons why the women weren't right for her, and in several cases she was correct. But even when the woman was very compatible, Sandra felt herself withdrawing.

Until Sandra went to therapy she did not understand how profoundly she had been affected by the death of her test pilot father. She had been "Daddy's girl," and was only five when he crashed during a training flight.

Sandra's mother did not comprehend the impact of this devastating loss on a child so young, and when she remarried a year later, she not only encouraged Sandra to accept her husband as a new father, but discouraged talking about her real father at all. Her mother and stepfather seemed to live only for each other, and Sandra's grief was compounded by even greater loneliness. In the reality of Sandra's inner world, being loved and special creates the anticipation of loss and loneliness.

By appreciating the depth of her unresolved childhood grief, Sandra has begun to trust and learn to be close again.

Valid Reasons Not to Commit to a Relationship

Sociopathic personality. Some individuals are not capable of true relationships. These people are sociopaths without conscience who exploit others for their own needs. They are delightful but dangerous seductresses who tell us everything we want to hear. They move from place to place, job to job, relationship to relationship. Be aware that no amount of love, no depth of understanding, can transform a sociopath. Such women are incapable of normal love, no matter how attractive or charming they appear to be.

Four years ago Topaz was seen at all the parties with an actress from a repertory company in a nearby city. "So this is the one, Topaz?"

"Yeah, this is it!"

Last year Topaz was going out with Phoebe, a high-powered lawyer who was involved in a major case that attracted wide publicity.

This year Topaz brought out Marion, a straight woman who had been married to a wealthy businessman. They were seen everywhere in Marion's new red BMW convertible. They traveled to Europe and skied at Aspen.

Topaz collects trophies. She inflates her sense of self-importance by how her lovers look, how much money they have, and their social visibility. While her prey may be seeking love, she feeds on their talents and public image. These are not relationships. They are conquests.

Addictions. Drug and alcohol addictions are illnesses that render a woman incapable of a respectful commitment. While these addictions are active the substance, not other people, is the central focus of the woman's life. Women who have been in a recovery program for more than a year begin to work on relationships that are honest and mutually giving.

Childhood abuse. Women who are survivors of severe childhood abuse, particularly incest, and who have not yet dealt with their feelings about the abuse, or who are just beginning treatment, would be

wise to wait before making a serious relationship
commitment.

Most relationships suffer severely or break up
during the emotional storm of memories, flashbacks,
projections, and deep pain that come up during treatment. It is a double injustice that women who are
denied emotional safety and comfort in childhood
must also forgo the pleasure of adult relationships
until they undo what was done to them.

Timing. Someone may be right for the relationship, but the time in her life is not. For example, in
the first few months after a breakup most people
crave support and affection. These needs may make
them want to connect to someone new, but they
would be connecting through anguish and pain. Only
as the grief subsides is a space created for a new
love to grow.

Death of child or parent. The death of a child
or of a parent creates a profound grieving process. In
the first year after such a loss the person is
essentially unavailable to begin a new commitment
because she is not emotionally present. Bereaved
people speak of feeling as if they are sleepwalking.

While a woman experiencing such a loss might
appreciate warmth and caring, she is temporarily less
capable of attaching emotionally to another person.

Traumatic loss. Traumatic losses include those
of friends, siblings, and past lovers. Death is always
difficult, but if someone has experienced a loss
through such things as suicide, murder, national
disaster, or airplane crash, a deep shock is created
that makes the person emotionally unavailable. For a
while, an individual's sense of safety in the world, or

of being able to predict what will come in the future, is shattered.

Power motive. The morning after Connie's first date with Justine, she called her friends to say, "She's young, but she has so much potential."

Connie began a My Fair Lady fantasy in which she saw herself teaching Justine how to dress and how to get a promotion. In short, Connie would make Justine over to become all that Connie could envision for her.

Connie does not love Justine. She loves the feeling of power she gets from creating a new person. Connie hides her motive even from herself by thinking about how wonderful the results of her evolutionary plan will be for Justine.

Compelling need. Help could be needed for many reasons, including financial support for herself, assistance with raising children, access to citizenship, entry to career opportunities, help during illness. This compelling need and the response to this need can create a powerful bond, which may temporarily feel as intense, or even more intense, than love and compatibility.

Pressure to be in a relationship. Lesbians feel less pressure to enter a relationship prematurely or inappropriately if they have a rewarding social life as a single person. This often requires the lesbian community to become an even more loving place, where single women are supported and included.

Are single women in your community and your personal social group included and supported?

If you are presently in a relationship, use the following checklist to increase your awareness of this issue.

Couple's Awareness Checklist — Attitudes
Toward Singles

	YES	NO
1. I have single friends.	☐	☐
2. My lover and I sometimes invite a single friend to socialize with us.	☐	☐
3. I would feel threatened if my lover spent time with a single friend.	☐	☐
4. I think my lover feels threatened if I spend time with single friends.	☐	☐
5. One of the reasons I started my relationship when I did was because it is hard to be single in our community.	☐	☐
6. When someone I know is going through a breakup I am available for support.	☐	☐
7. When we are planning for holidays or special occasions we think about who is single and include them.	☐	☐
8. Since we have been a couple we feel we don't have enough in common with single women.	☐	☐
9. When our social group plans an event, I would expect single women to be included.	☐	☐
10. I believe some single women actively try to break up couples to start a relationship of their own.	☐	☐

KEY If you answered *no* to **6 or more** of the above, you are living your life primarily in a couples world. You and your partner might like to consider how you feel about the status of single women in your community. If there is anything about that status that you or your lover would want to change, consider the following actions:

- Work toward the attitude that maintaining your relationship is a joint responsibility. If a single woman outside can threaten it, then you need to strengthen your relationship.
- Talk together with your partner about what you want your policy as a couple to be about including single people in your social life.
- Identify what you have in common with a single woman rather than how you are different.
- When someone in your community breaks up, call, make a plan to see her and, if you enjoy her company, continue to contact her after the first month of her acute pain. If you or your partner feel threatened, see her together, at least part of the time.
- Seek out singles at social events. It is often easier for a couple to approach a single woman than the other way around.

Single women often say that when their friends get into relationships they join a world of couples and the friendship is lost. This separation of singles and couples in the lesbian community can be caused by the intensity of the early stages of a lesbian relationship, which largely excludes anyone outside it. There is also a perceived threat — consciously or unconsciously — felt by some women in couples. Also, the separation may be caused by assumptions made by singles themselves.

If you are presently single, use the following

checklist to see if you are contributing to your lack of contact with women in couples.

Single's Awareness Checklist — Attitudes Toward Couples

	YES	NO
1. When I am thinking of sharing an activity with someone, I consider inviting a friend who is part of a couple as well as a single friend.	☐	☐
2. When a friend becomes part of a couple, I expect that we will continue to spend time together.	☐	☐
3. When a friend becomes part of a couple, I make an effort to get to know her partner.	☐	☐
4. I invite couples to my home.	☐	☐
5. I would be comfortable going out with a couple.	☐	☐
6. I sometimes invite a couple to share an activity.	☐	☐
7. I would be comfortable in a group of couples if at least one other single person were present.	☐	☐
8. I would try to see a couple, or a friend who is part of a couple, on a weekend.	☐	☐
9. I think of my friends who are in relationships as separate people as well as half of a couple.	☐	☐
10. I see the similarities between myself and my friends who are in couples, as well as the differences.	☐	☐

KEY If you answered *yes* to **3–5** questions, review your *no* answers. Ask yourself if your assumptions about interacting with couples are based on actual experiences you have had. Perhaps you are limiting your social life unnecessarily.

If you answered *yes* to **0–2** questions, ask yourself if it is your preference to avoid relationships with couples or if you feel uncomfortable with them. If you are uncomfortable and would like to change the situation, you might select a couple with whom you feel the safest, and who you know socializes with singles, and reach out to spend time together.

If you have a friend whom you trust and who is part of a couple, try talking to her about your discomfort. Many women in couples neglect single friends out of a lack of awareness, and they become more responsive when the issue is brought to their attention.

Reasons for entering a relationship may be conscious or unconscious. Ask yourself the reasons why you are seeking, or are in, a relationship. If it is in order to fill the empty space in your life and make living worthwhile, what other qualities are you bringing to the relationship that will make it mutually rewarding for both of you?

Understanding your wants, needs, and motivations in seeking a partner will enable you to bring to the relationship your true self and realistic expectations of all that the relationship can be.

Chapter 3:

Why Does Sex End?

True mutual satisfaction characterizes a good sexual relationship. If both women are aware of what they want sexually and are experiencing it, they need not look further. For some couples this is the reason sex — meaning full sexual expression — may end. Each lesbian couple has a style of sexual expression that is specific to the relationship. Lesbians who by conscious choice do not include active sexual behavior in their lives should not be seen as limited.

That said, the perception that it is inevitable that lesbian relationships eventually become sexless is open to challenge.

When sex ends for some lesbian couples, they are

content enough with the other rewarding aspects of their relationship to stay together. Others break up and move on to relationships that include sex, at least for a time. There are also lesbian couples who are not sexual and want to be, or who are sexual and would like to increase or improve their sexual relationship.

If you would like your sexual relationship to be different there is action you can take. Following are the eleven reasons that may cause sex to end even though the couple would like it to continue. In each case, there are three aspects to the situation — awareness, assessment, and action.

Awareness includes recognizing what dissatisfaction, if any, you experience in your sex life.

Assessment encourages you to notice how you feel about what you have discovered. How important is it to you to make a change? Are either of you willing to make a change?

Action offers specific suggestions on how to achieve the goal you select.

1. Newness Ends

The fact that a lover is new and unknown enhances sexual excitement.

Fusion. In the beginning of sexual and emotional intimacy there is a moment when each woman experiences the dissolving of a barrier between herself and her partner. There is a fusion, a sense of becoming one.

This fusion can be and often is part of a sexual experience, although it does not occur only on a sexual level. In some sense, in that moment the two become one person. The awareness that in some basic way we are alone, disappears. The universal human anxiety of being separate from all others, and therefore vulnerable, is soothed. People talk about feeling as if they are completely inside the other person, and of wishing to always feel this way.

Intimate knowledge. During the initial coming together, women share their histories, feelings, dreams, private information about their bodies, and their reactions to family and friends. It is as if each is saying, "Here is everything I know of myself at this moment, and I share it with you."

The process of sharing is exciting, and the sense of knowing another so completely creates a satisfying sense of intimacy. The excitement of intimacy is dynamic, not static. Basically, the process of sharing depends on the process of discovery.

A relationship strategy common in the forties and fifties was to maintain an air of mystery, not to be known completely. This was particularly recommended to women to maintain a lover's interest. This strategy implied that a woman should dole out information about herself sparingly, so it would last. Ongoing personal growth was not an expectation.

The sixties and seventies brought experimentation with openness to feelings, self-exploration, and sharing in relationships. For a time people felt a greater sense of freedom, an increase in sexual openness, and an emotional high from knowing themselves and others more fully.

This period culminated in the extremes of the eighties and nineties, when the tendency was to reveal all personal details publicly as well as privately. The purpose of this excessive public exposure seemed to be to shock and to receive attention. The difference between a personal relationship, in which intimacy was created by being known completely, and a less personal relationship was blurred by television talk show acknowledgment of personal pain and extreme behavior.

This social backdrop influences women in their personal decisions about how much to reveal about themselves. Each woman needs to determine how much she will share with her partner and at what pace this information will be revealed. As a couple, there should be agreement about how much will be shared with others.

In order to experience the closeness and excitement that intimate knowledge brings, two things are necessary. To a certain extent intimacy implies exclusivity. We are known intimately by only a few people — perhaps only one person. When everything is known by everyone, no one is special.

When both women in a couple continue to grow and change, the process of discovering a new lover is ongoing. "I share with you the person I am today. Tomorrow I am in some way new, because life continually changes us." Your challenge in keeping a relationship dynamic is to be aware of the changes in you as they occur and of your emotional reactions to these changes. This information is a continuing source of intimate knowledge.

It is common for couples to experience intense intimacy at the beginning of a relationship, although not all couples who are in satisfying relationships have this experience. Those women who do not may question their relationship.

Lana and Elaine have been together for eight months and see each other as possible permanent partners. They both love country western dancing, they enjoy sex, and they would like to raise a child together.

In relationships with others in the past, both women have had experiences that began with lusty sex that was overwhelming for at least the first three months. Their relationship did not begin this way, and both Lana and Elaine wonder if it is a bad sign.

Lana and Elaine originally worked together. It was Lana's first job after high school, and after a year she transferred to another office to receive a promotion. They continued their friendship over the next year and became closer when they both got involved in country western dancing. After attending a gay pride festival at the same time, they discovered an attraction and began seeing each other.

Because Lana and Elaine knew each other as coworkers and friends, they did not experience an initial intense unfolding of information. Although they missed out on this highly charged experience, they have a level of knowledge and intimacy gained over a period of time that provides a sound foundation for a relationship.

Physiological changes. The difference between the heady excitement at the beginning of a relationship and the change that takes place as time progresses is well documented.

The body chemistry of a person in the first intoxicating stages of love differs from the later, steadier warmth and intimacy that develops over time. At the beginning of an intense relationship, each lover's body is flooded with a chemical very like amphetamine, which creates a feeling of well-being, joy, and vitality.

As the relationship progresses, another group of chemicals takes over — the endorphins. These promote feelings that are steadfast, ardent, and deeply rewarding.

2. Risk of Revealing Your True Self

It is a universal longing to be known completely by another person and to be loved and accepted with that full knowledge of your true self. At the same time, the impulse to reveal creates anxieties about how we will be received when all is known.

A loving relationship is one in which an atmosphere of safety is created over a period of time. Safety means, "I will not judge you or leave you because you tell me who you are. I will learn to take responsibility for my reactions to who you are."

Both women long for, and are committed to, a level of intimacy where each person both knows the other and is known by her. This process happens in a manner that fits the two individuals, occurring at their own pace and in their own way.

In order to become more skilled at self-revealing, you need to learn to manage the discomfort you feel about what you anticipate will be your lover's response. Here are two steps that can help:

Step 1: Identify how you *imagine* your lover will respond.

If I am open and honest, I'm afraid she will:

- Laugh at me
- Criticize me
- Put me down
- Ignore me
- Humiliate me
- Judge me
- Leave me
- Tell others what I have shared
- Withdraw emotionally
- Get angry
- Some other response

Once you have identified your fear, check it out with your partner by saying something like, "Sometimes I want to tell you what I'm feeling, but I'm afraid that you'll put me down if I do," or, "I'd like to get closer to you but I think you'll think less of me if I tell you how I feel inside."

It is very likely your lover has had some of the same fears and will fully understand your anxiety.

Step 2: Identify how your family responded to you. One of the reasons people anticipate a certain response to self-revealing is that their families responded to them in that particular way when they were growing up. Think back to your childhood and remember how your family reacted when you revealed something about your true self.

When I showed my feelings to my family, they:
- Supported me
- Distracted me
- Got angry
- Shamed me
- Seemed uncomfortable
- Punished me

- Comforted me
- Offered me food
- Humiliated me
- Mimicked me
- Ridiculed me
- Shared similar feelings

As you think back, you may realize that your family had different reactions to different emotions.

In addition to whatever programming you received in your family, experiences with teachers, friends, and past lovers may also have shaped your expectations. In order to accurately experience your current partner's responses, you need to distinguish her feelings and actions from what the past has led you to expect them to be.

3. Inhibitions

It is difficult to grow up inhibition free in a culture that gives women so many conflicting messages about being sexual, where women's sexuality is defined by advertising executives, and when rape and incest are common.

By the time a woman begins an adult relationship, her attitude about sex has been influenced by her family, religion, school years, culture and society, and she may not have had any meaningful conversations about sex. She may have experienced multiple sexual traumas. Because of the many meanings attributed to a women's sexuality, she is rarely encouraged to observe herself and learn in an open and free atmosphere what she is like sexually. For these reasons many women are inhibited in the sexual sphere of their lives.

Even more so, lesbians may have struggled against, and actively repressed, their sexual feelings before they accepted themselves as lesbians. Their inhibitions may prevent them from moving seductively, from speaking in a sexual manner, from engaging in sexual behavior that interests them, from delighting in the sight, smell, taste of their own bodies or their partner's, or from being able to request what they enjoy.

One of the reasons that sex ends in a lesbian relationship is that the initial passion is unable to permanently dissolve the inhibitions that exist in one or both women. As passion subsides to an everyday, though enjoyable, level, it is no longer enough to prevent the acquired inhibitions from blocking sexual behavior.

Any sexual practices that are not physically or emotionally harmful are normal. This certainly does not mean that women have to enjoy or participate in all sexual behaviors — only those that are acceptable to them. However, if a woman is unable to consider or imagine a particular sexual behavior, if a one-time experiment is considered wrong or disgusting, if a woman tightens inside when talking about sexual possibilities, or if a woman views her feelings, fantasies, or bodily functions as wrong or revolting, it is likely that she is sexually inhibited.

4. Affection Is Enough

Holly and Pat are breaking up. They have realized that they want different things in life and are ending after two years of living together. Holly says, "The hardest thing to give up is the touching."

Pat agrees. "We sleep together so well! I love to cuddle up to Holly and drift off."

"We hold hands all the time," says Holly.

"I'm really going to miss the sweet little kisses for no reason," says Pat regretfully.

Many lesbian couples rate their affection as the most important part of their relationship and feel satisfied physically without excitement and orgasm.

Two things are important in assessing the impact satisfying affection has on a relationship:

1. Lesbians and lesbian couples must say what constitutes a satisfying relationship for *them*. Lesbian sexual satisfaction should not be defined by comparison with gay or heterosexual relationships. Such comparisons imply that other relationships are right or complete and that lesbian relationships are lacking in some way.

Susan E. Johnson's research on long-term lesbian relationships shows that nearly 60 percent of lesbians in long-term couples are very satisfied with the sexual relationship they have with their partners. "Being satisfied does not necessarily mean being very sexual." (*Staying Power: Long Term Lesbian Couples*, p. 156)

2. Through self-awareness and open discussion between lovers, lesbian couples need to declare their

needs and preferences for affection and sex. If a need for sexual contact is denied, it is likely that an attraction to another woman will eventually develop. Women's skill in adaptation must be balanced with the ability to be assertive.

5. Anger

Sex may temporarily stop, or even end permanently, because of the way one or both women handle anger. Some women actively withhold sex because they are angry, and some women are unable to feel turned on or be sexually vulnerable when they have these intense negative emotions.If you are less interested in sex than usual, or less responsive to your partner, here are some ways to discover if anger may be contributing to the change:

Anger Checklist

	YES	NO
1. In general I hold back from my lover what irritates me.	☐	☐
2. Recently I have held inside the things my lover has done that irritate me.	☐	☐
3. I sometimes think, "I'll fix her."	☐	☐
4. After she has hurt me, I enjoy the thought of hurting her back.	☐	☐
5. When she has hurt me I believe she deserves to be punished.	☐	☐
6. If I'm angry at her, I feel good when she approaches me sexually and I don't respond.	☐	☐

7. My parents were cold to me when they were
   angry.   ☐ ☐
8. When I'm hurt or angry I become cold and
   distant.   ☐ ☐
9. I keep a mental account of what my lover
   has done that I don't like.   ☐ ☐
10. I enjoy stories in which people get even.   ☐ ☐
11. When my lover is angry with me I feel
    uncomfortable being open sexually.   ☐ ☐
12. When my lover is angry with me I want
    to protect my body and my feelings.   ☐ ☐

KEY If you answered *yes* to **any** of the 12
questions, it is possible that anger is affecting your
sex life.

If you answered *yes* to **5 or more** questions, your
relationship is being negatively impacted by anger
and your sex life is very likely to be affected.

If you answered *yes* to **8 or more** questions the
way you are handling anger is definitely an issue in
your relationship.

6. Dominance–Submission

Some clinical research suggests that dominance
creates sexual excitement. Dominance includes a wide
range of attitudes and behaviors, and for a number of
women dominant or submissive roles are their primary or exclusive way of relating sexually.

The idea of dominance is offensive to some
women for political reasons, while others find it

frightening to think of giving up control to their partner. For some the fantasy of being dominated is titillating, as it means having no responsibility for what happens, so it is, in a sense, freeing. Being dominated can also bring feelings of safety and protection, thus allowing sexual openness.

Some women enjoy occasionally playing a dominant role because it allows them to feel powerful and to express an aggressive side of themselves.

Lesbians who are comfortable with some degree of dominance and submission describe their experiences as pleasurable with high levels of sexual energy. It is crucial that *both* women willingly embrace their roles and agree to the extent that each will express dominance and submission.

There are a number of ways of adding an experience of dominance and submission to your sex life:

Teasing. The essence of teasing is to show or tell your partner that you've got something that will make her feel really good, but she can't have it . . . yet. To want something, yet not have it, creates a heightened emotion that is a combination of longing and frustration.

Yolanda and Nikki are cooking dinner together in their apartment. Yolanda brushes her breast against Nikki's arm. Nikki responds by reaching out to touch it, and Yolanda pulls back playfully. "Uh-uh. Not until I have my dinner."

After dinner Yolanda walks into their living room and takes off her sweater. Topless, she sits on the couch. When Nikki walks over, obviously enjoying the sight of Yolanda's breasts, Yolanda teases, "Why don't you make me a cup of tea? I'll be needing my tea before I can think about anything else."

Yolanda and Nikki both enjoy the buildup of sexual anticipation that teasing brings.

When Nikki returns with tea she sees that Yolanda has placed a vibrator next to the couch. Yolanda laughs suggestively. As they begin touching and stroking, Yolanda whispers in Nikki's ear, "It's going to make you feel so good . . . but . . . not yet."

Role-playing in fantasy. Some couples do not enjoy dominant-submissive behavior, but share fantasies with a dominant-submissive theme. They might turn each other on by describing their fantasies and then making love, or sharing the story during lovemaking. The fantasies could include such things as one overpowering the other, begging for sexual satisfaction, or using physical restraint. Many couples find that these fantasies are fun and greatly heighten sexual feelings.

Role-playing behavior. Costumes, tone of voice, vocabulary, and sex toys/items can enhance the dominance-submission theme. If she feels this way, it is important that a woman is able to tell her partner that she might want to experiment with spanking, with dressing to suit her role, or with being talked to in a dominant way. Talking about these behaviors needs to be handled nonjudgmentally, with the requirement of physical and emotional safety and a mutual goal of increased sexual pleasure.

Viewing videotapes. Adult video stores and video catalogs offer lesbian videotapes with dominance-submission themes. Some women are more stimulated by what they see than what they hear, and some women are more comfortable observing dominant-submissive behavior, rather than participating in it.

7. Boredom

Doing the same thing the same way leads to boredom in any aspect of life, including sex. People tend to do what is familiar for many reasons: It eliminates the anxiety of what is new; it is comfortable; they lead demanding lives that don't allow time or energy to experiment; they are lazy; they are afraid of criticism, failure, or looking foolish.

Doing the same thing feels safe, but ultimately is less interesting. Doing something new feels stimulating and yet requires more of an investment. For many lesbian couples a combination of familiar sexual behaviors with some variation creates a balance of comfort and discovery.

Sylvia and Dinah have been lovers for five years. They live in neighboring communities and spend weekends at Sylvia's apartment. They generally attend temple services together on Friday evening, make love Saturday morning, walk their dogs and do errands Saturday afternoon, and play poker with friends Saturday night. Sunday they relax, visit family, and cook dinner together before Dinah returns home.

They are content and both agree that Saturday morning is their favorite time for sex. Last month

Dinah called Sylvia and simply said, "Meet me at the Highway Motel Wednesday night at eight. You won't regret it."

They both enjoyed the break in their routine and felt more passionate the following Saturday.

Keeping Boredom at Bay

Any change can decrease boredom. Here are some possible changes that can help keep boredom at bay:

- "I always come first. I'm going to do you first this time."
- Have sex in a room in which you never have before.
- Find a way to have sex outdoors.
- Have sex in the shower or tub.
- If you don't usually do this, share a fantasy.
- Read to each other from a lesbian novel, book of poetry, or book about sexual behavior.
- Eat dinner naked.
- Bathe your partner.
- Spend at least one night of your vacation some place other than your home.
- Volunteer to house-sit; make love in someone else's home.
- Play music during lovemaking, if you usually don't.
- Have a picnic on the floor of your living room and make love right there.
- Send her a love letter.
- Rent movies that turn you on.

- Experiment with sexual behavior you haven't tried before, like body painting, stimulation with vibrator, penetration with a dildo, foot massage, or stroking with feathers or silk scarves.
- Talk during sex if you usually don't, telling your lover what is turning you on.
- Make sounds that express your pleasure if you are usually silent.
- Use explicitly sexual vocabulary if you usually don't. You might say "suck me" or "do me" or "lick my pussy."
- Change the position you customarily use during sex. Visit your local bookstore for a book on lesbian sexuality if you need ideas.
- Be willing to try something new. You don't have to give up your favorite and familiar ways of having sex. You should not do anything that offends or terrifies either you or your lover, but remember that it can be fun to do something just because it's new.

Creating Anticipation

Close your eyes and remember a time when you just met someone who attracted you very much. Remember how you felt the sexual energy. Perhaps you danced together at a party or went for coffee and you felt very aware of your body and of hers as you talked about movies and thought about sex.

You made plans to see her in a few days and you wondered, "Will we? When will we? Where will it happen?" In the middle of your workday you found yourself smiling as you undressed her in your mind.

While looking forward to an experience we create a picture of what it will be like and begin to have anticipatory feelings about it.

There are a number of ways to create anticipation:

- Plan a future joint activity. Talk about it in terms of being sexual.
- "Let's go camping next weekend. Let's be sure to pack some of our oils."
- "I like the strawberry..."
- Shop together for a sex toy.
- Send your partner a sexy card or note in the mail. End your message with an invitation, "Let's spend Sunday morning in bed" or "Wear my favorite T-shirt tonight."

The anticipation becomes part of the sexual experience and is likely to increase the intensity of excitement.

8. Failure to Maintain Attractiveness

Each partner in a relationship has a responsibility to maintain a level of attractiveness. Of course, this is not to say that a woman should conform to society's definition of attractiveness or that she should have any image other than the one she chooses to have, but it does imply that attractiveness is a valid issue in a relationship and needs to be addressed non-defensively.

Janine and Kate have been feeling distant from each other. During the first two and a half years of their relationship they were content, but recently Kate has been dissatisfied.

Kate: I want to tell you something, Janine. Please don't feel criticized. It's important.

Janine: What, honey?

Kate: Well, it's about your attitude lately.

Janine: What attitude?

Kate: When we started living together, you seemed to love life. You'd sing around the house. You were seeing your friends a lot. There hasn't been much of that for a few months.

(Janine looks crestfallen.)

Kate: I knew this would upset you.

Janine: It's okay. Go ahead.

Kate: Your energy really turned me on. I miss it.

Janine: I guess I've been kidding myself about how much my job has been bothering me. I know I haven't been myself lately . . . and I'm afraid to think about looking for another job.

Kate: We'll do it together. I know there's a great job out there just waiting for you.

Attraction is influenced by superficial issues like grooming and hygiene, as well as by deeper matters such as character, vitality, and accomplishments. The

most important point is that women be able to say
what is affecting their sexual desire, irrespective of
whether it is superficial.

Discussions about attractiveness must be handled
with sensitivity, not only to personal feelings, but to
each woman's cultural and social background and
politics.

Why you are discussing attractiveness needs to be
clear. It is not to criticize or to impose one person's
values on the other. The intention behind the discussion is to keep the relationship vital.

The following checklist may help you increase
your own awareness about your feelings concerning
attractiveness and could be the basis of a conversation with your partner.

Attractiveness Checklist

	YES	NO
1. I have been influenced by my culture and the media to see female attractiveness in a defined way. Have I really thought through what I consider attractive in myself, women in general, or my lover?	☐	☐
2. Do I allow myself to be aware of what makes me feel sexually attractive?	☐	☐
3. Do I allow myself to be aware of what is sexually attractive about my lover?	☐	☐
4. Which of her characteristics best defines who she is? Is that characteristic attractive to me?	☐	☐
5. Do I know what it is about the way she interacts with other people that attracts me sexually?	☐	☐

6. Do I know the ways she treats me that attract me sexually? ☐ ☐
7. Do I have a healthy and realistic attitude about weight? ☐ ☐
8. Do I spend some time each day attending to my hygiene and appearance? ☐ ☐
9. Do I dress in a way that pleases myself? ☐ ☐
10. If I knew a way I could dress to turn my lover on, would I sometimes please her this way? ☐ ☐
11. Do I accept compliments? ☐ ☐
12. Do I tell my lover when she is attractive to me? ☐ ☐
13. Have I come to terms with the strengths and flaws in my appearance? ☐ ☐
14. If I wanted to make a request about my lover's appearance, would I be willing to? ☐ ☐
15. If my lover made a request about my appearance, would I be willing to listen and consider making a change? ☐ ☐
16. Do I accept that everyone's sexual interest is affected to some extent by physical appearance? ☐ ☐

9. Difficulties in Initiating Sex

"I really enjoy sex once I get into it. It's just not my style to get things started."

Gina's comments reflect how many women feel about initiating sex. Women's socialization teaches us to *react* to the needs of others rather than to initiate behavior on the basis of our own needs and wants.

When this style of relating is taken into the sexual arena, there are often difficulties in initiating sex.

Difficulties with initiating need not be viewed as an insurmountable barrier to enjoying sex. Learning to initiate involves awareness and willingness to change. Awareness comes from noticing your thoughts and feelings when you consider initiating. These may include the following, as well as others:

- No one is making the first move.
- I'm not used to making the first move.
- I feel awkward making the first move.
- I am frustrated with our sex life.
- I want to have an enjoyable sex life.

Willingness means, "I don't *want* to change but because I'm dissatisfied I'll give it a try." When you are willing you move out of your usual way of being in order to gain something of importance to you.

Willingness could include the following, as well as other statements that fit your particular situation.

- I'm willing to try, even though I'm uncomfortable.
- I'm willing to learn, which involves experimenting.
- I'm willing to feel my emotions while trying something new.
- I'm willing to be awkward until the new behavior becomes familiar.

Willingness is an internal experience. Change, in this case, is internal and behavioral. Possible changes might include:

- I will not let my family's view or society's
  view of assertive behavior in women
  prevent me from changing.
- I can view a woman who initiates sex as
  feminine.
- I can enjoy the process of change.
- I can enjoy taking charge of my sex life.
- I can make the first step verbally.
- I can make the first step physically.

Signaling

One form of initiating lovemaking is to send a signal.
It can be behavioral or verbal. A signal is an indirect
way of saying "Let's make love" that is understood
by both women.

Charlotte is a shy woman and feels restrained
about mentioning anything she wants. She enjoys oral
sex. When she wants Genevieve to go down on her,
Charlotte, who usually showers in the morning, runs
a bath. Genevieve understands Charlotte's shyness.
The two of them established this signal after they
had been together several years when Genevieve
noticed that Charlotte seemed tense and blushed
when asked why she was taking a bath rather than a
shower.

Their signal works as well as words and now
creates a sense of anticipation in them both.

Verbal signaling. Verbal signaling can include
using affectionate or sexual nicknames, speaking in a
sultry voice, commenting on each other's appearance,
mentioning missing each other, suggesting spending

time alone, or perhaps using a word or phrase you
have agreed will mean you want sex.

Behavioral signaling. Behavioral signaling can
include touching each other's breasts or genitals,
open-mouth kissing, being undressed when she
wouldn't expect you to be, dancing closely or
sensually, flashing, or drawing your partner near you
or on top of you.

Some women are reluctant to signal because of
the fear of rejection. It never feels good to be rejected; however, it is important to decrease sensitivity to
rejection. Here are some attitudes that will help you
become more accepting of the possibility.

- Have the attitude "Nothing ventured, nothing gained."
- If you are signaling to someone new, the
  sooner you find out whether or not she is
  interested, the less time you waste.
- Someone has to take the initiative. She
  may be interested but more frightened
  than you.
- If you are in a relationship and your partner doesn't respond, it is likely that she's
  not interested at that particular time,
  rather than that she's plain not interested.
- Work toward developing an internal convic-
  tion that you are an attractive sexual partner rather than depending on someone
  else's responses to reassure you of this.
- Try to enjoy signaling as the first step in
  a pleasurable process. Don't view it as a
  test of your personal sex appeal.

Actions to Take

Review the past week, the past month, the past year. Make an effort to get a sense of the whole relationship. Who initiates sex? How do you let each other know you want to be sexual?

Following are some ways to initiate. Because you're making a change, expect to be clumsy some of the time. Try to sample several of these suggestions, bearing in mind that feeling uncomfortable is often part of doing something new.

Make reference to spending time alone. "Could you come home early tonight so we can be together?"

"Let's not make plans for Saturday night so we do what comes naturally."

"Could you skip your workout tomorrow morning so we could stay in bed together?"

Suggest showering or bathing together. "Is there room for two in that shower?"

"I just ran a bath. Want to join me?"

Suggest shopping for something related to sexual pleasure. "While we're here renting a video, how about checking out the adult section?"

"I've got a catalog here that sells sex toys. Why don't we look at it together?"

"I've always wanted to see you in black panties. Let's buy some."

Make a change in what you wear to bed. If you usually wear a T-shirt to bed, wear nothing. If you usually wear nothing, put something on.

"Why are you wearing that?"

"I thought you might like taking it off . . ."
Suggest the pleasure of touching. "I would love it if you'd stroke my back."
"Your skin feels so good when I touch it."

10. Health Problems

A lessening of sexual desire, a decrease in lubrication, or any physical discomfort during sexual activity could be a sign of a physical change or a health problem.

It is important to have a relationship with a physician or nurse practitioner with whom you can openly discuss changes related to sexuality. If you are embarrassed to bring up the topic, it is good to let your health-care provider know that you are uncomfortable and then state as directly as possible the changes you have observed. It is appropriate to ask, "What health conditions could be contributing to this change?"

Personal Health Checklist

	YES	NO
1. I have a physician or nurse practitioner who is my primary health-care provider.	☐	☐
2. I have a physician or nurse practitioner who specializes in gynecology.	☐	☐
3. If I were concerned about my health affecting my sexuality, I could talk to my health-care provider about this.	☐	☐
4. I could talk about sexual matters with a health-care provider if a supportive person		

came with me. I have someone I could ask
to come along. □ □
5. I am aware of how my menstrual cycle affects
my sexual feelings. □ □
6. I have had a physical examination in the last
two years. □ □
7. I have an annual gynecological examination. o o
8. If I have chronic health problems, I have a
system to manage them. □ □
9. When I have an acute illness I take measures
to correct it. □ □

KEY Each *yes* answer increases the likelihood that
you will manage your health in a way that supports
a good sex life.

Review your *no* answers. Make a plan to take
better care of your health. Seek support from friends
and family. If fears about coming out to health-care
providers are interfering with your seeking care,
approach lesbian organizations for assistance in
finding providers who are lesbian-friendly.

11. Butch–Femme

Role-playing has often been mentioned as part of
lesbian lifestyles. Particularly before the seventies, the
terms *butch* and *femme* were used to describe lesbian
behaviors.

By describing butch-femme as roles that are
adopted much as donning a costume, perhaps we are
missing an important issue of butch-femme identity
that affects sexual interest — what you *are*, rather
than how you *act*.

During the intense years of the feminist movement all women's roles were scrutinized for their
limiting effects, including butch-femme in the lesbian
community. Many lesbian women who identified with
feminism moved away from the structured butch-
femme roles. Some lesbians found the change freeing,
while others felt judged and were constrained from
continuing in relationship patterns that had been
previously fulfilling.

Billie laments that her girlfriend wanted to make
a lot of changes. She says, "We were doing just fine.
I've always been a butch, and I know what I need.
We couldn't keep it together after a while. But I
have a fine woman now. A real femme. We understand each other."

Debate continues as to whether butch-femme
refers to an aspect of identity — that is, who a
woman actually *is* — or if these are simply roles
which can be adopted, changed, or discarded.

Sharon Gedan says, based on my clinical experience, I believe that styles of sexual expression are
part of identity, and that women who resist exploration of their personal sexual style will either have
limited sexual relationships, or relationships without
sex. Know who you are, be who you are, and sex is
more likely to flourish.

It seems to me that there are some lesbians who
have a clear butch identity and some who are clearly
femme. For those whose identity is butch, they may
have a forceful presence, or not — may show their
butchness in dress, or not. Who we really are is
defined by what is inside, not by external appearances.

In the same way, femmes may be flamboyantly

feminine, or not. It isn't what is on the outside which is the defining factor, but rather how an individual lesbian experiences her lust, sensuality, vulnerability, and the manner in which it is natural to express them.

Other lesbians find in themselves a combination of butch and femme characteristics, some perhaps more pronounced than others, or there may be an interesting blend that allows initiative and response to comfortably cohabit.

If a lesbian cannot experience her sexual energy and desire in a way that is genuine because it is "too butch" or "too femme," she is cutting herself off from what is natural inside of her.

If either or both partners in a relationship are unaware or uncomfortable with whatever active or receptive sexual energy occurs within, then the natural flow of energy between them will be blocked.

Exploring one's own sexual identity needs to be done without judgment of how butch or femme one may be in general, or in a given moment. Freedom of expression preserves sexual interest and sexual energy.

If You're Not Having Sex and Would Like To

Many relationships drift gradually away from sex. If a woman in such a relationship would like to turn the tide, she may feel uncomfortable about starting a conversation on the subject, thinking, "What if she's not interested? What if the current state of affairs is okay with her? It's been so long. How do we get started if we both want to try again?"

Remember that your partner may also want to talk about sex and may be feeling even more anxious than you are. Sharing your own feelings and observations can be a good way to begin:

"I'm sad that we don't get sexually close any more. Would you mind if we talked about it?"

"We seem to be drifting away from each other sexually. If you said today, 'Let's go right up to bed,' I don't think I'd be ready, but I'd like to talk with you about it."

If it took you time to drift apart, it will take time to find your way back. Keeping expectations realistic will help prevent anxiety. For some couples, spending relaxed time alone together is a good starting point.

Conversations aimed at reconnecting often include commenting on what you've always enjoyed about your partner, such as, "You have the softest skin. I would never get tired of touching it." Or, "I remember the first time I saw you smile. It makes me feel just as warm inside today."

When you first talk about reconnecting, it is best to state willingness and positive intentions and to allow some comfort with the topic to develop before talking about problems.

If the change in sexual contact between you is sudden, it is best to be direct: "We've had sex twice a week all the time we've known each other, and now we haven't even come close for a month. Can we discuss it?"

Any conversation about a change in sexual contact needs to be done without blaming or criticizing. A question like "Why don't you make love to me any more?" creates defensiveness, while the better phrased "Something is different for us sexually — can we talk?" invites discussion.

The most important thing about a sexual conversation is to *start* it. Talking does not obligate either of you to be sexual, but it does create the likelihood that you will be close and will make considered decisions about your sex life.

Chapter 4:

How to Develop a Loving Relationship

It is possible for anyone to develop a loving relationship; however, women who were raised by loving adults can more easily be loving partners than those who experience loving relationships for the first time as adults.

Irene was raised by her mother and grandmother, who filled her childhood with love and laughter. She saw her father every other weekend and talked to him nightly before bedtime. "It's easy for me to show how much I love Vivian. I saw love and felt love all around me when I was growing up."

Tanya and Christie have lived together for four

years. "I am like the professional dancer who didn't take lessons until I was eighteen," Tanya explains. "The kids who started at three or four had a huge advantage over me, but I worked hard and caught up. I knew I had deep feelings for Christie, but I had to learn how to show them."

Six Requirements

Being able to develop a loving relationship involves six requirements.

1. Information and examples. If you come from a loving family, much of what you need to create a loving relationship as an adult was learned in your early years. Even troubled families demonstrate some behaviors that are helpful in adult relationships. You might review for yourself who the significant adults were in the first seven years of your life and what each of them taught you about being caring and supportive. Remember that whatever bad examples you saw are learning experiences of what *not* to do.

2. **Willingness to be vulnerable.** Opening your heart and letting your partner know how you feel about her makes you vulnerable to possible hurt or rejection. However, it also opens the door to closeness and deep caring. Women are often exquisitely sensitive to their partners, and this sensitivity can create one of the most delightful aspects of lesbian relationships — the sharing of sweet and tender moments.

3. **Prior experience.** It would be rare for someone's first attempt at a relationship to be a deeply loving one. Dating and early relationships offer

the opportunity to learn about sharing, coping with differences and conflict, and getting a real sense of your own needs.

When early relationships end, they should not be considered failures. At the end of a relationship, review what you want to do differently next time. Janet says, "When I was a teenager I always hoped the first real relationship I had would last forever. Now that I'm living with Claudia, I realize what I learned in my two earlier relationships have made it possible for me to have a really good one with her."

4. Willingness to learn from mistakes. We expect Olympic athletes to hone their particular gifts through trial and error. In the same way, though gifted at relating, women need the freedom to experiment and learn from what works and what doesn't. Relationship difficulties and endings need not be viewed as failures, but rather as opportunities to become more skilled at the business of loving.

5. Willingness to practice loving behaviors. Pam calls Lynn once a day from her law office to tell her how her day is going. "I didn't share enough with Lynn the first year we were together, and that kept us from being close. If I did share, it was mostly details. I had to write myself notes — 'Call Lynn' — and I had to remind myself to say how my day made me feel. It's still not natural, but it's getting easier."

JoAnn put her fist through a wall during her first argument with Betty. "My temper scared her. At first I told her, 'That's just me. Get used to it.' But I love her, and that wasn't right. I talked to my minister, and she had some good ideas. Whenever I start to get mad, I count to ten. Sometimes I count to fifty or say a prayer or take a walk. Then we can talk. I can tell that Betty's a lot happier."

6. Awareness of differences. When you are developing a relationship, the most common cause of conflict and misunderstanding occurs because of the differences between you. It is easy to understand the motivations and decisions of a partner who is similar to yourself. But because you cannot enter the heart and mind of someone very different, you will misinterpret the reasons for her behavior.

If you are different in such things as how much time you need to spend together, how verbal you are, how you handle conflict, or how you express affection, you are likely to experience frustrations as you develop your relationship.

Clear, honest communication is the remedy and will help you to avoid seeing a difference as a deliberate attempt to annoy or upset you.

Six Stages of a Relationship

Although there will be some variety in the way relationships develop because of the personalities of the women involved and the life experiences each has had, there are six distinct stages. The particular pleasures and challenges of each of these stages can be predicted. Information about these can help you both expect and deal with forces that otherwise might be frightening, confusing, or destructive.

Stage one: The first three months (*Hoping for the best*). This is the exciting stage where you have positive feelings that this woman may become very important to you. It is a time when the focus is on similarities. Generally at this stage, both you and the other person will be

- On your best behavior
- Sharing what you want her to see
- Projecting onto her what you need and want

During stage one, neither of you is deliberately trying to be false, it is just that there is not enough time to develop an intimacy in which all the realities about each other can be known and experienced.

WARNING: If you make a serious commitment in the first three months of a relationship, you are doing this on the basis of very limited information. There may be some disturbing discoveries ahead.

Stage two: The three-month point *(Break or make time).* This stage is a brief one that occurs at approximately three months into a relationship. Reality has started to break through and your view of the previously "ideal" woman becomes modified by things you don't like and behaviors you find disappointing or frustrating. In essence,

- Strengths and weaknesses become apparent
- You realize the ideal person doesn't necessarily have all the hoped-for qualities

It is during this time that many relationships break up under the weight of reality. Many people want the fantasy person they had for the first three months and won't accept the actuality. Others simply lack the maturity to deal with the fact that there are differences.

In stage two we confront the reality of other people and our interactions with them. The challenge is to see if we have in ourselves what it takes to deal with differences, weaknesses, and disappointments, as well as all the positive things relationships bring to us. It is also a time when we must learn to communicate much more fully about what is happening and how we feel about it.

NOTE: The three-month point in a relationship is often a crisis time. Those women who have had a long history of three-month relationships are showing that they prefer fantasy and cannot tolerate reality in another person.

Stage three: Three months to one year *(Learning to deal with realities).* The pleasure of stage three is a deepening of the relationship: The challenge is to deal with realities. This is when you learn what it is like to be with her in a wide variety of situations. During this stage, each woman,

- Experiences both the positive and negative aspects of the other's personality
- Accepts that there are differences
- Starts to come to terms with a full picture of the relationship

Stage four: One to three years *(Consolidating the relationship).* The consolidation stage begins about the end of the first year and lasts until approximately the three-year point. It might seem surprising that it takes at least three years to really know another person, but there are many aspects to personality and it takes time to be presented with a wide variety of situations in which you see her respond to you, to others, to stress, to change, to joy.

After approximately three years it is likely that you will feel you know the other woman well and can predict what she will say or do. You will also have worked out coping strategies for dealing with differences between you.

The pleasure of stage four is an increasing feeling of security and comfort. The challenge is to communicate as fully and as nonjudgmentally as possible. A woman who is successfully navigating stage four might say, "I have learned that I can be me and that I can be loved as myself." This creates a richness and depth to the feeling of being loved and of loving someone else.

Stage five: Three years plus *(A stable base for a full life).* Stage five begins at three years and continues throughout the life of the relationship. The pleasures of stage five are related to realizing your life goals and dreams, which may include enjoying career success, having a home, pursuing interests individually and as a couple, bringing up a child, providing community service, developing spiritually.

A challenge is that boredom may creep in on an emotional or sexual level or that partners may create such a routine together that they feel bored with their life in general. You can combat boredom by actively seeking stimulating life experiences and by promoting growth as individuals and as a partnership.

A second challenge is that obstacles may block the achievement of your goals and dreams. Many couples find that there are emotional and financial challenges to achieving life goals, and that communication, plan-

ning, and determination are required to fully enjoy
the satisfactions of stage five.

Stage six: At any time *(The end)*. Stage six is
the end of the relationship. One woman may die, or
there may be a breakup of the partners. However the
relationship ends, the challenge will be to deal with
feelings of loss and grief and the new beginning that
will follow.

Certainly with the death of a partner there is
enormous grief, and it can be difficult at times to
recall all that was good and positive. Similarly, the
breakup of a relationship brings anger, disappointment, and frustration. Even so, there are few
relationships in which there has been no pleasure and
no learning, so it is possible to recall the past and
appreciate the pleasure you felt then.

Relationship Traps

There are certain times when you might be
particularly vulnerable and might therefore make
unwise decisions about relationships because you
haven't taken into account the impact certain life
experiences have on you.

Following a breakup. The more significant a
relationship was to you, the more dangerous is the
immediate time afterward in terms of starting a new
relationship. In the first few months after a breakup,
both women are hurting, angry, and especially vulnerable.

Because you are likely to feel so emotionally
needy after breaking up, there is a tendency to fill

the empty space with *anyone,* rather than to choose an appropriate partner from a place of strength.

If this substitute partner is particularly good at nurturing wounded feelings, this will feel very good for the moment, but there is no guarantee that she has the qualities you need when you are emotionally healed.

Following a partner's death. As with any devastating loss, a grieving period must be experienced and worked through when a partner dies. The consensus is that it requires a minimum of a year to grieve a death, and if your relationship was a particularly long one, it will take even more time. This doesn't mean you have to limit meeting new people, but it is advisable that you emphasize friendship and connect with loving, supportive people rather than begin a new love relationship in the first year of grief.

After the death of a parent. People often get into relationships they later regret during the three months to a year after the death of a parent. It doesn't matter how old you are when your parent dies, it will always have a profound effect. Parents are the people who support and guide us, and we may initially feel adrift and too readily seek an anchor. Once our parents are gone we are much more aware of our own mortality and feel a need to grab life while there's still time.

Because of the deep nature of this grief, people often seek comfort. They reevaluate their lives and consequently become concerned about what they have accomplished, so they may hastily make a commitment. If you are in this situation, consider giving yourself the time to grieve before making a decision about a serious relationship.

If it is your partner who has lost a parent (or someone else very significant to her), you will notice changes in her behavior. A grieving person will often lose interest in sex, will become more remote, will seem preoccupied. Understandably, her joy in life and her ability to interact in a fun and sexual way will be greatly reduced, at least in the short term.

During menopause. Both partners should have accurate information about the effects of menopause. This can be a baffling time. Some women have few symptoms, yet for many there will be appreciable physical and emotional changes. Some women will become depressed, occasionally to a serious level. Until menopause is regulated, lovemaking may be uncomfortable because of a decrease in vaginal lubrication.

It is important to remember that menopause is a transition time and that a woman has several management options, including hormone replacement in consultation with her physician, or following a regimen of exercise and diet supplements.

At any time of significant change. People often fall into traps at times of significant change in their lives. Significant changes include: new job; physical change due to some kind of body-altering surgery; move to another locality; large adjustment in financial status.

These are danger periods because such changes often bring about emotional upheaval. Beginning a relationship during these times may provide some comfort and pleasure, but will subject the relationship to considerable, if not fatal, stress.

Steps to Take Before Considering a Serious Commitment

Unless the woman you are seeing is purposely trying to mislead you and is very skilled in deception, you can get the information you need before making a serious commitment with the following steps.

Allow enough time. There is absolutely no substitute for time. It doesn't matter if you are a therapist, a psychiatrist, a psychic, a genius — it makes no difference at all. You have to have enough time, and it *must* be more than three months.

Be willing to observe. This means that, no matter how strong your feelings of excitement or pleasure are, you still have to do basic observation of how she looks, talks, and acts. Watch for any inconsistencies — these are clues that something may be wrong.

Be willing to share your wants and needs. This doesn't apply to the first date, but over a period of time it is essential that you let her know what you need and want from a partner. This is the only way you can find out if she will be responsive to you. Do *not* wait until after you have made a commitment to begin to share these aspects of yourself and your life.

Actively listen to her. In the same way that you should be willing to share your wants and needs, you should listen to the other person to hear what she is saying about her wants, needs, goals, values. Many people are surprised how much there is to learn if they just stop talking and listen.

Observe how she is with other people. Do

you like the way she interacts with other people? Does she have the social skills that are important to you? Would you be satisfied in being treated the way she treats other people? Ultimately, *that is the way you will be treated.*

Face squarely the information you are getting. You can be very excited and captivated by her and not want to squarely face the information you are getting because you feel you will have to let go, and that means you will be disappointed. In order to prevent heartache, you *must* look at the information. Short-term disappointment is nothing next to the emotional upset of a bad relationship.

Have enough wisdom to know why you're staying with her. Ask yourself some hard questions: "Am I staying with her because I don't want to be alone? Because it's socially acceptable to have a partner? Because I want someone, anyone, to share my life?" If these are your reasons for developing a relationship, you are limiting yourself and your partner from experiencing the full rewards of sharing love and mutual goals.

One of the reasons you might continue to stay is because you suffer from low self-esteem. It would be useful to learn whether you value yourself enough to seek the relationship you really want. There are books and workshops that will help you gain self-esteem.

If you are staying with her just to have a relationship — *any* relationship — then understand the negative implications this has for your future happiness.

If you are thinking about making a serious commitment, a number of signs will tell you that you're on a good course. Don't be intimidated by the following precommitment checklist. You don't need to be perfect, nor does your potential partner. Use the checklist as a basis for discussion.

Note that the first ten questions cover areas that are extremely important to the health of your relationship.

Precommitment Checklist

	YES	NO
1. I have dated her for more than three months.	☐	☐
2. When we talk I feel understood.	☐	☐
3. We have at least one important thing that we share.	☐	☐
4. We have similar needs and beliefs about being out.	☐	☐
5. When we argue, we reach a resolution of the issue.	☐	☐
6. I have a sense of what trouble spots in our relationship we will need to work on.	☐	☐
7. I believe I will work at whatever difficulties present themselves in our relationship.	☐	☐
8. I believe she will work at whatever difficulties present themselves in our relationship.	☐	☐
9. I can be myself with her.	☐	☐
10. We have the same beliefs about monogamy.	☐	☐
11. We are able to talk about our sexual relationship.	☐	☐
12. We laugh together.	☐	☐

13. We each have someone to go to for guidance
    if we're having difficulty.   □   □
14. If we weren't lovers, I would choose her for
    a friend.   □   □
15. We have time to spend together.   □   □
16. We each have our own friends.   □   □
17. I understand and accept her need for time
    and activities away from me.   □   □
18. She understands and accepts my need for
    time and activities away from her.   □   □
19. I understand what her life goals are.   □   □
20. I know what my life goals are.   □   □
21. Our life goals, though not necessarily the
    same, are compatible.   □   □
22. We are comfortable with at least some of
    each other's friends.   □   □
23. We understand and accept what is impor-
    tant to each other for holidays and special
    occasions.   □   □
24. We are sexually attracted to each other.   □   □
25. I enjoy making love to her.   □   □
26. I enjoy the way she makes love to me.   □   □
27. We have fun together.   □   □
28. I can tell her when I want or need some-
    thing from her.   □   □
29. I notice that she tells me what she wants or
    needs from me.   □   □
30. I have seen her stressed or upset.   □   □
31. She has been around me when I have been
    stressed or upset.   □   □
32. We each understand what helps the other
    when we're stressed or upset.   □   □
33. We both know how to compromise.   □   □

34. I have an effective way of taking care of my
health. ☐ ☐
35. She has an effective way of taking care of her
health. ☐ ☐
36. We have discussed our individual financial
situations. ☐ ☐
37. We have a plan for handling our finances
after we make a commitment to each other. ☐ ☐
38. I have a relationship with my family that
works for me. ☐ ☐
39. She has a relationship with her family that
works for her. ☐ ☐
40. We understand and accept the kinds of contact we will be having with our respective
families. ☐ ☐
41. We have talked about what is important to
us spiritually. ☐ ☐
42. We have the same beliefs about having
children. ☐ ☐
43. I feel secure with her. ☐ ☐

KEY For questions 1 through 12, each *no* is worth 3 points. For questions 13 to 43, each *no* is worth 1 point. Add your points.

0–10 SOLID GROUND to make a commitment. Work together on the questions to which you answered *no*

11–20 SHAKY GROUND to make a commitment. Work together to increase your *yes* answers

21–30 SERIOUS SITUATION. Unwise to make a commitment until you significantly improve your *yes* answers

31–67 STOP. You're making a mistake.

Ten Ways to Create
a Loving Atmosphere

Once a commitment is made, the following ten guide-
lines will help you create a loving atmosphere within
your relationship.

1. Make her feel special.
2. Be aware of people and experiences that are
   important to her.
3 Remember what is happening in her day or week
   and ask about it.
4. Focus on her needs as well as on yours.
5. Accept her efforts to make you feel special and
   loved.
6. Accept her compliments.
7. Be affectionate.
8. Make humor a part of your interactions together.
9. Have time alone with each other each week.
10. Develop your personal way of celebrating the
    special times in your relationship.

The element that overrides all others in developing a loving relationship is *time*. There is no substitute for it. Lesbians enter relationships like swimmers
pushing through surf and waves to get to the deep
waters quickly.

Why do lesbians rush into intimate relationships?
Because women are so capable of, and interested in,
relating, there is a rapid development of intimacy and
a feeling of having known the other woman for a
long time.

This is an illusion. No matter how good women are at communicating, no matter how many nights they stay up talking about their pasts and future hopes, there is only one way to get to know another person, and that is through the passage of time.

Chapter 5:

Sexual Communication

Sexual communication between lesbians can be transmitted on verbal, physical, or energy levels. It can be a direct request, a suggestive glance, an invitation conveyed by a bodily movement. It can be heard, seen, or sensed. It can be an expression of something you feel, something you want, or something you want to give to another. It can be an expression of "I love you" or "I want to be close to you" or "I want to meld with you" or "I want to get off." Sexual communication can be the deepest expression of your particular female style.

Sexual communication is first shaped by the guidance you received in your family about sexual

matters and the emotional atmosphere in which that
guidance was given. Think back to your early years.
Was there a feeling of naturalness related to sexuality
or one of discomfort? Could you ask questions and
express feelings? Was your development as a woman
welcomed? Were you appropriately protected and
taught self-respect?

Society expands on the education begun at home.
Women learn from what they observe and how they
are personally treated. One significant contributor is
the confusing examples of female sexuality in the
media. Female sexual "ideals" of appearance and
behavior contradict each other — underweight waifs,
blatantly sexual singers and actresses, androgynous
women, and women who are routinely brutalized by
their partners.

The path to a clear and comfortable identity as a
woman and as a lesbian can be difficult and may
require a process of self-observation. This includes
sorting out the external influences from your own
genuine reactions and being willing to accept and
support the true self that you discover. A sense of
one's identity as a woman and lesbian is the basis of
sexual communication. "This is who I am, what I
feel, and what I need."

If both women are interested in identifying their
true sexual responses and styles of expression, an
atmosphere needs to be created in which exploration
can take place. For many couples, sex becomes better
over time, and it should be expected that trial and
error will be part of the process.

A sexual fit includes finding positions and movements that create a body fit; learning each other's
styles of initiating, becoming excited, and experiencing

orgasm; mapping each other's bodies to maximize sensual and sexual pleasure; appreciating times of day, week, and month that you are each likely to be more sexually stimulated; discovering the varieties of sexual behaviors that are fulfilling, that are favorites, and that are unacceptable.

Things to Talk About

While you are on your sexual journey, you will need to talk about a number of things.

Discussing the parts of your body that feel particularly good when they are touched. This could include what feels comforting, nurturing, relaxing, mildly stimulating, and sexually exciting. If you don't already know, you can find out together by touching and talking. It's a good idea to experiment: "Touch softer or harder," "Take more time with that," "Touch me with your fingers/hand/cheeks/breasts/mouth/toes . . ."

Discussing whether you like talking to be part of sexual interaction. This could include sharing your reactions to what you are experiencing, talking to your partner in sexual language to increase excitement and tension, exchanging compliments or loving thoughts, sharing sexual fantasies, talking playfully or jokingly, sharing thoughts and feelings that emerge in the close moments after orgasm.

Telling each other what doesn't work. You need to remember that even very good lovers cannot be completely tuned in to their partner's needs, so they require feedback. However sensitive, skilled, and

observant you are, you don't live inside your
partner's body.

**Overcoming your reluctance to participate in
sexual behaviors that your partner enjoys and
that you would not select on your own.** Your
reluctance could come from a range of things —
embarrassment, shame, lack of skill, lack of interest,
selfishness, rigidity, self-centeredness. If your partner
is not suggesting something that is dangerous to your
health or well-being, you might try talking through
your feelings with her, or even with a counselor, in
order to develop a willingness to respond to her
needs and perhaps expand your sexual repertoire in
the process.

Creating a system that keeps sex fresh. You
will need to talk about your openness to literature,
music, films, and videos that could be sexually stimulating. It is useful to discuss where and when you
have sex. Can these patterns be changed to introduce
variety? Are you open to trying a different position, a
sex toy, or a different style of dressing or talking
that could stimulate your partner? Make a plan to
try something different, and afterward discuss how it
affected your sexual interest and satisfaction.

**Noticing the vocabulary you use with each
other.** Is it clear? Is it sexy? Does it seem stilted or
medical? Do you both understand the words you are
using? Are the words a turn-on? A turnoff? Tell each
other any way you would like to change or improve
your sexual vocabulary.

**Being aware of whether you are honest with
your partner about what you like and what you
would like from her.** If you are hedging, withholding information, or minimizing what you want,

ask yourself why. Do you feel entitled to sexual satisfaction? Are you protecting your partner and thereby not giving her a chance to satisfy you? Do you feel your needs are too great or abnormal? Are you attempting to manipulate your relationship by giving your lover a false impression of you or your satisfaction with the relationship?

Sharing information about how you like to climax. Most women have a preferred or habitual way of having an orgasm. You and your partner might also enjoy exploring alternate ways of climaxing. You are more likely to feel satisfied and your lover is more likely to feel successful, if you let each other know what works the best and feels the best.

Sharing information about what turns you on. You may have some of this information from self-exploration or from prior experiences with another partner. It's possible you can discover more of what turns you on with your current lover. The more information you share with her, the better chance she has of satisfying you.

The following is a checklist that may increase your awareness of your particular turn-ons. If you have a lover now and would feel comfortable sharing information with her, you might use the checklist as a basis for conversation.

Sexual Turn-on Checklist

Check the statements that are true for you.
These are the times in my life I have felt the most sexually turned on:

☐ The first three months of a new relationship
☐ A few days before my period

☐ After a romantic date
☐ While listening to music
☐ When my partner talks sexy to me
☐ When I read a story with a great sex scene
☐ When I watch someone dancing in a sexy way
☐ When I see my partner all dressed up
☐ After dancing
☐ When we take a bath or shower together
☐ When my partner teases me and makes me wait
☐ When I imagine doing something sexual that I would never really do
☐ When I masturbate
☐ When I watch my partner masturbate
☐ When we have been apart for a while and get together
☐ When I feel that I'm in charge of what's happening
☐ When I feel that she's in charge of what's happening
☐ When we have phone sex
☐ When I watch someone flirting with my partner
☐ When she takes me by surprise
☐ When I've spent the day in the sun
☐ When we've been involved in physical activity
☐ When I feel that my lover is turned on
☐ When we have oral sex
☐ When my lover stimulates my breasts
☐ When my lover stimulates me anally
☐ When I observe my lover in a powerful situation like handling something difficult or being successful at work
☐ When we go away together
☐ When I feel that we've broken a rule
☐ When we feel really close
☐ Other

Problems in Sexual Communication

"I can't orgasm . . ." It is important to remember that climaxing is a skill, and skills are developed. As with any skill, some women orgasm more readily than others, but any woman can learn.

Women who have not yet learned to orgasm can find methods for increasing excitement by exploring their bodies on their own or with their partners. Helpful steps to take might include reading *For Yourself* by Lonnie Barbach, Ph.D., working with a therapist experienced in sexual counseling, or talking to a physician or nurse practitioner who specializes in gynecology and has experience in sexual counseling.

"I'm worried. Something's changed . . ." Changes in a sexual relationship are inevitable. When they occur, communication is essential. The most important thing to remember when a change occurs is, *don't panic.* Change is something to be interested in, not feared.

A good way to begin the conversation is a simple statement like, "I've noticed a change between us sexually. Have you?"

It is helpful to be specific about the change, such as, "We don't seem to take as much time as we used to," or "I miss the times we'd have spontaneous sex."

It is very important to avoid judging or blaming each other. Most people feel at least somewhat sensitive about sex, and feeling judged or criticized will lead to defensiveness and will almost guarantee a breakdown in communication.

Examples of judgmental or blaming comments are, "You're not as sexy as you used to be"; "You're obviously not interested in sex anymore"; "What's wrong with you lately? You used to be spontaneous about sex."

Your attitude in approaching the problem is vital. "Something's changed; let's try to understand" is a great deal more likely to lead to constructive communication than "Something's wrong; one of us is at fault."

"Statistics don't lie ..." Some couples create anxiety in their sexual relationship by competing with statistics: "Mary told me they've had sex every day since they met!" or "I read that couples our age have sex on an average of three times a week."

Find your own individual sexual rhythm and the natural rate of frequency for the two of you. Comparisons can lead to feelings of inadequacy or disappointment in one's own sex life. Support what is natural to the two of you, and your feelings of satisfaction will increase.

"I've been sexually abused ..." Sensitive communication about sex is particularly important if either of you is a survivor of sexual trauma, such as rape, incest, sexual harassment, or any other sexual experience involving force. These negative experiences are likely to impact a woman's ability to be vulnerable, to trust, to be open, or to be sexually assertive.

Partners of survivors of trauma need to learn not to take personally their partner's reactions that come from past painful experiences.

Survivors need to understand their reactions in order to communicate to their lovers what comes from this relationship and what comes from the past.

Many couples find it useful, if not essential, to read about recovery from sexual trauma, to use workbooks, to attend support groups for both survivors and partners, and to seek counseling.

This is not an impossible situation. However severe the trauma, it is definitely possible to work out a good sexual relationship in the present. Your communication is likely to be effective if you understand how the trauma affected you, if you both can support whatever feelings arise from the past, and if you allow time and space in the relationship for these feelings without either of you judging yourself or each other.

"This is embarrassing, but ... " Some sexual issues are difficult to talk about. Anything that makes a woman feel sexually inadequate is likely to have a negative influence on communication.

Wanda and Phyllis have been involved for seven months. During the first two months, they spent more time in bed than out of it. Since then, they have had sex infrequently, and they are starting to fight about insignificant things. One evening they talk about the situation:

Phyllis: Want to fool around?
Wanda: Not really. I'm kind of tired.
Phyllis: It's only eight o'clock.
Wanda: Why don't we watch a movie?
Phyllis: Let's make our own movie ... about two sexy women.
(Wanda is quiet and looks uncomfortable.)
Phyllis: Something's wrong, isn't it?
Wanda: Kind of.

Phyllis: What is it? Honey, we've got to be able to talk. Are you interested in someone else? Is that it?

Wanda: This is pretty embarrassing.

(Phyllis cuddles up to Wanda.)

Wanda: It's about when I go down on you.

Phyllis: What about it?

Wanda: Well, my other lovers always seemed to love it . . . and I really like to do it . . . But I can't seem to turn you on or satisfy you. I feel like I'm not a good lover anymore.

Phyllis: Is that why you've been staying away from me?

Wanda: I didn't want to feel like a failure.

Phyllis: I do like what you do. I guess I should have said something. Sometimes I'm afraid that I'm not clean and I might taste bad and I tense up or try to distract you.

Wanda: You always taste good!

Phyllis: I'm not really comfortable with oral sex. I'd like to be.

Wanda: Want to take a bath together . . . ?

Nina and Helen had known each other for four months when they moved in together. They are very attracted to each other and have wonderful sex several times a week. On Nina's birthday Helen surprised her with a beautifully wrapped package hidden under the covers. Nina gleefully opened her gift and found a vibrator, something they had never shared. Helen watched as Nina went from laughing and excited to stunned and withdrawn.

Helen: Whoops. Did I make a mistake here?

Nina: Whatever made you think I'd want one of these?

Helen: I thought it could be fun.

Nina: We were doing okay on our own.

Helen: Why don't you like vibrators?

Nina: It's not natural. I want you to want me, not some mechanical thing.

Helen: I *do* want you, Nina, a lot. It's just a toy, honey, something to play with once in a while. I never meant to hurt you. I'm really sorry.

Nina: How does this thing work, anyway?

Helen: Here's how you turn it on.

Nina: Yikes! Does it hurt?

Helen: You've never tried one?

(When Nina shakes her head, Helen smiles.)

Helen: Want to try it once? If you don't like it, I'm calling Goodwill.

Nina: I don't know. It's kind of scary.

Helen: Here, try it on me, so you can see what happens.

Nina: Okay, here goes. I guess you'll keep us from getting bored.

In both examples these women were willing to share feelings and their true thoughts and reactions about what was making them uncomfortable. Open communication helps a couple move forward into an even deeper and more rewarding relationship.

"I'm sorry, I just can't talk about it..." Because sexual adequacy and sexual behaviors are sensitive subjects, defensiveness can be triggered to the point that sexual communication breaks down.

Martha and Kelly are spending Saturday evening at Kelly's apartment. They have been seeing each other for three months and have set the evening up to have an opportunity to be sexual.

They have both been thinking about sex during the week, and Martha is nervous. She wants to have a conversation with Kelly about talking during sex and about sometimes talking with a sexy tone. She wants the talk to go well because she likes Kelly a great deal.

Kelly lights candles and they share the salad she made and the chicken Martha brought with her.

Martha: I've been thinking about you all week.
Kelly: (moving closer) I hope you've been thinking about the same thing I have.
(They laugh and kiss. Martha musters her courage.)
Martha: Kelly, I started talking sexy to you when we were making love the other night... And I thought maybe it bothered you.
Kelly: Do we have to talk about that?
Martha: Well, I was just wondering... It turns me on to talk sexy, and —
Kelly: Do you have to spoil a nice evening?
Martha: I didn't mean to spoil anything. Why are you getting so upset?
Kelly: I just don't want to talk about it, okay?
Martha: I'm sorry I brought this up.
Kelly: I'm sorry you did too. I thought we were going to have a romantic evening.
Martha: We still could.
Kelly: I really don't feel like it.

Strong, sudden reactions and closing doors to communication indicate a raw emotional nerve has been touched. If you have such reactions, you will

need to sort out your feelings yourself or with the
support of friends, spiritual guides, or a counselor.

If your partner reacts with a communication shut-
down, it is best to (a) temporarily back away from
the subject, (b) acknowledge that something painful
has been touched upon, and (c) express the hope that
you can continue talking about the issue at another
time

"Have I told you how great it is?" When
women talk about a good sexual relationship, they
usually mean that it gives them pleasure and a sense
of well-being, it releases tension, it makes them feel
closer and known more fully. Some women experience
a spiritual openness during sexual exchange, and
many women feel their loving and trusting feelings
are deepened.

How would you rate yourself as a sexual communicator?

Questionnaire on Sexual Communication

	YES	NO
1. I am willing to talk about sex with my partner.	□	□
2. I have a sexual vocabulary that my partner understands and that is comfortable for me.	□	□
3. I believe it is my responsibility to let my partner know what feels good to me.	□	□
4. I am willing to let my partner know how I like to climax.	□	□
5. I would tell my partner if something was uncomfortable or unacceptable to me.	□	□
6. I am interested in listening to my partner talk about her sexual likes and dislikes.	□	□
7. I believe that a good sexual relationship re-		

quires talking, experimenting, and giving
each other feedback. □ □

8. I am open to trying safe sexual behaviors
that my partner suggests. □ □

9. I know that my partner cannot read my
mind and that she needs me to communicate
what does or doesn't work for me sexually. □ □

10. I can show my partner what I enjoy. □ □

11. If a sexual behavior is physically uncomfortable, I can let her know. □ □

12. I can tell her my sexual fantasies. □ □

13. I can comfortably refer to the parts of my
body. □ □

14. I can comfortably refer to the parts of her
body. □ □

15. I know what is sexually exciting to me. □ □

16. I can tell my partner what excites me. □ □

17. I am interested in what excites and satisfies
my partner. □ □

18. I know what turns me off sexually. □ □

19. I am willing to tell my partner what turns
me off. □ □

20. I am willing to observe my sexual feelings
and responses in order to understand myself
more fully. □ □

21. I can initiate sex when I want to. □ □

22. I can tell my partner when I don't feel like
having sex. □ □

23. I am accepting and nonjudgmental about
myself sexually. □ □

24. I am accepting and nonjudgmental about my
partner sexually. □ □

25. I am an active participant when we have
sex. □ □

26. I can move my body and make sounds of pleasure during sex. ☐ ☐
27. I think about ways to create variety in our sex life and tell my partner what I am thinking. ☐ ☐
28. I am willing to experience sexually stimulating music, movies and videos and share my responses to them. ☐ ☐
29. I can tell my partner what I find sexy about her. ☐ ☐
30. I can tell myself what is sexy about me. ☐ ☐

KEY If you answered *yes* to **20 or more** questions, you are an excellent sexual communicator.

If you answered *yes* to **11 to 19** questions, your communication has room for improvement.

If you answered *yes* to **fewer than 10** questions, your relationship is being limited by your communication blocks. Talk with your partner about the need for a specific plan to open your sexual communication.

If you decide that you need to work on your skills in sexual communication, the first step is to make a commitment to the effort. The second is to set a specific goal. You might use your *no* answers to help with goal setting. For example, if you answered *no* to Question 16, "I can tell my partner what excites me," you might set one of the following goals:

- The next time we're making love, right at the time that it's happening, I'll say, "That feels good."
- When I see her tonight, I'll say, "You

know how you were touching my breasts
this morning? It was great."
- I'll leave her a note saying, "Wear that
perfume again soon. It turned me on."
- I'll call her today and say, "I really liked
last night."

Remember that goals are about what you are
going to *do*. When you are working on your goals it
is okay to seek whatever support helps you be a
more effective communicator. You can work toward
change on your own; you can ask for your partner's
advice and encouragement; you can seek help from
friends, family, religious or spiritual advisors, or a
counselor or therapist. Choose whoever is comfortable
to talk with and helps you work realistically toward
your goal.

Talking About Safe Sex

Rae and Danielle are seeing each other for the third
time. Danielle tells her friend Kate, "She's making
dinner for me. I am so turned on I couldn't sleep.
Tonight's the night. The only weird thing is, I guess
we have to have The Talk."

"Birth control?" asks Kate with raised eyebrows.

"Very funny." Danielle makes a face. "How
unromantic to ask, 'By the way, Rae, have you got
any STDs?' "

"How are you going to approach the subject?"

"I've been giving it a lot of thought. I'm going to
say that we have a nice thing started here and I
don't want to do anything now that will spoil it

down the road, so I want us to talk about how to keep each other safe from disease."

Kate grins and points at Danielle. "What if she wants *you* to get tested?"

"I think we both have to have an AIDS test before we get into the good stuff," says Danielle firmly.

"What if Rae decides you're talking about safe sex because you've slept around a lot?"

Danielle spreads her hands. "She'd be wrong."

Kate gives Danielle's shoulder a comforting pat. "She'll probably think you're very cool."

Pilar and Mary have lived together for five years. Pilar has genital herpes, and Mary has not become infected. Their friend Bonnie also has herpes and is just starting a new relationship.

Bonnie: This is pretty personal stuff, but I know you guys have been dealing with this for a long time. Any advice?

Pilar: Be honest with your girlfriend, and be aware of when you're getting an outbreak. I can tell when I'm getting one. Can you?

Bonnie: Pretty much.

Mary: You know she can get it from you before the sore comes out, don't you?

Bonnie: Yes, I knew that. I can usually feel it for a couple of days before I get the blisters.

Pilar: That's a really contagious time.

Mary: The first year we were together, I was so nervous that I almost wished I'd just go ahead and get herpes so I could stop worrying about it.

Pilar: So you haven't told Susan yet?

Bonnie: I'm going to tell her today. Do you think she'll want to know all the details of what to do?

Mary: I know *I* did!

Pilar: Mary and I are always really careful. We use separate towels and I wear underpants to bed if I have an outbreak. And I watch my stress.

Mary: Remember when your mom was really sick? We weren't sure she was going to make it . . .

Pilar: And I had three outbreaks of herpes in a row.

Mary: Don't get discouraged, Bonnie. You can still have a great sex life.

Bonnie: Thanks for talking to me. It really helps.

Talking about safe sex includes four things:

1. Sharing information about which sexually transmitted diseases (if any) you now have

2. Listing which medical tests you've had that indicate whether you are disease free

3. Determining what medical information you need to be clear about your health

4. Agreeing on which techniques you will use to prevent transmission of disease

The anticipation of talking about safe sex is usually worse than the conversation itself. Having the conversation is a caring act. If your partner does not view it as caring, or is unwilling to share information, you are in an unsafe situation and should consider avoiding sexual contact with her.

Gonorrhea, chlamydia, and syphilis infections are quite rare in lesbians who are sexually active with women only. If you or your partner have had sex with men, it is possible to transmit these diseases.

Chlamydia often has no symptoms and can be detected only through medical testing.

Genital warts (HPU) and herpes (HSV) do occur in lesbians who have had contact only with women. Herpes can be spread by oral-genital contact or genital-genital contact. Once you have herpes, you have it for life.

Genital warts (HPU) are much more likely to come from heterosexual contact, but cases have been reported in lesbians who are sexual only with women. Genital warts are a risk factor for cervical cancer, making regular testing by Pap smear essential.

If you or your partner experience genital itching or have odorous discharge, it could be an infection, and both of you should have a medical check.

Any risk of transmitting the HIV virus (which leads to AIDS) *must* be taken seriously. If you do not know your HIV status or that of your partner, you should avoid contact with all internal secretions and all blood, whether from menstruation or wounds. Contact should also be avoided with breast milk and any sores on the genitals.

Women who are seeking artificial insemination should be sure that the sperm donor has been tested twice for the HIV virus, the tests being three to six months apart.

Dr. Marjorie Angert, medical specialist in gynecological services for the city of Philadelphia, reminds her patients that any break in the skin is an entrance for the transmission of disease. Because nails can cause tears in the vaginal area, wearing a latex glove during penetration provides protection. Gloves can be purchased in a drugstore and can be used with over-the-counter lubricant jelly.

Dr. Angert notes that although plastic wrap is sometimes advised as a barrier, she is concerned about keeping the covering in place during sexual activity. She suggests a female condom instead.

Dr. Jo Ann Rosenfeld, who teaches and practices in Tennessee, emphasizes that the most serious risk to lesbian health is not disease but avoidance of health care. Lesbians have either had negative medical experiences or fear that they will have these experiences, and so many will put off routine check-ups or early attention to problems.

Information is usually available within the lesbian community about physicians or nurse practitioners who are either lesbian or supportive of lesbians. However, since more and more health care is provided through managed-care organizations, and since many women's choices are limited, it may become necessary to come out to health-care providers. If a care provider responds with judgment, anxiety, hostility, or unwanted mental-health referrals, it is important to request a referral to someone else: "This isn't working for me. I'd like to see a different doctor."

Health-care providers generally assume hetero-sexuality in their patients. Remember that the health-care provider works for *you*. Giving the physician information about your lifestyle offers the opportunity for more thorough care. Saying, "Doctor, my partner is a woman," will allow you to assess whether or not the physician is able to respond appropriately to you.

If you are diagnosed with a sexually transmitted disease, your physician will talk with you about diagnosing and treating your partner(s). If you have questions about your partner's exposure, it is appropriate to say something like, "My partner is a woman. Will this affect her?"

Although safe-sex conversations and use of safe-sex techniques are interruptions in the natural passionate flow of lovemaking, women feel less anxious about sex when safety has been established. There is no question that the discomfort that accompanies discussion of safety is minuscule compared to the disclosure that one has passed on a serious or fatal disease.

Chapter 6:

Preserving Love

Loving feelings originally occur spontaneously. Preserving love, however, requires attention and effort.

Seven Skills That Help to Preserve Love

There are seven skills whose use creates an atmosphere in which loving feelings are protected and in which they deepen. These are being present, communicating, managing or eliminating serious problems, extending beyond one's own comfort zone, maintaining perspective, creating and using adequate support, and dealing with conflict constructively.

1. Being Present

Being present creates an opportunity for interaction that is real, spontaneous, and fresh. It implies that you have an awareness of self and a willingness to share. A couple who can be with each other and a couple who are distant might actually spend time together in exactly the same way. The difference flows from the amount of contact each couple has. Contact includes touching and sharing of thoughts, feelings, and reactions.

Avril and Sherry talk about their eight years together. "Sherry is the first person I've been able to spend a lot of time with and not get bored. It's comfortable, and we can tell each other anything."

With another couple, Grace and Inez, things are very different. Grace tries to share her loneliness and sense of isolation with Inez. "We don't always have to be doing things. I'd rather we just spend time together, just hang out. I don't really get a chance to know what you're thinking or feeling. It's almost as if I miss you even when we're together."

Avril and Sherry feel enriched in each other's company. Grace feels deprived in her relationship with Inez.

A satisfying experience of being together is not dependent on the amount of time spent, although some couples report it takes a certain period of time to reach the state in which they feel relaxed and

open. This period can be used to shift focus from
work or other tasks to sensuality and sharing.

"Dominique comes home from work about six, but
it's like her body walks in the door and about an
hour and a half later, she shows up," says her
partner.

Olivia and Ursula spend Saturday morning
running errands and talking about work, finances,
and other practical matters. Saturday afternoons are
sacred. Olivia says, "We make lunch together and
spend a quiet afternoon. We don't even answer the
phone. Neither of us makes other plans for that time,
and if something interferes we really feel the
difference."

It is the sharing of self that creates the sense of
vitality and newness in a relationship. Because we
continually change and because life presents change
to us, there are new experiences and new reactions to
share. Couples may feel distant for a while and
wonder what is going on. It may be that one or both
women are experiencing a change that is not yet
completely in awareness or that is difficult to share.
Struggling to maintain self-awareness and taking the
risks inherent in sharing are the work of being with
your love.

In order to create an atmosphere in which sharing
is likely to occur, both women need to make time
available to each other, to learn to listen without
comment, and to manage their own reactions — which
might include fear, hurt, anger, or judgment.
Although it's sometimes difficult to achieve, the most
helpful attitude is one of being interested and
accepting.

Being with your love is not always comfortable.

The sharing may include information and insights that are challenging or painful, but the continuous unfolding of one human being to another will keep your relationship alive and growing.

2. Communicating

Couples who enjoy their relationships and feel successful in managing them mention good communication as their most important tool. Good communication develops from a willingness to take risks, communication skills, and practice. Becoming a good communicator is no different from becoming a good musician. Beginning with whatever natural ability you have, you practice — first the basics and then with greater range and variety as your skills increase.

Honesty tempered with sensitivity produces messages that can be received without the defensive barriers going up. The excuse "I was just being honest" is not an acceptable disclaimer for words that are overly aggressive or cruel.

On the other hand, "I don't want to hurt her feelings" does not excuse failure to communicate information that gives your partner a true sense of your joint relationship.

The challenge is often, "How can I express my true thoughts and feelings in a way that is considerate of you?" In order to practice sensitive honesty, you must know her well enough to identify what she is sensitive about and what she is not, and to distinguish her sensitivities from your own.

Constructive forms of communication include

- Sharing thoughts, feelings, information
- Acknowledging your partner and your relationship
- Problem-solving
- Making requests
- Offering support
- Sharing observations
- Creating an atmosphere that is playful and fun

Destructive forms of communication include

- Blaming
- Criticizing
- Humiliating
- Provoking
- Manipulating
- Shaming
- Minimizing
- Overreacting
- Intimidating
- Lying

As we grow up, communication skills can be learned from a variety of sources: family, school, reading, observation of effective communicators, workshops, therapy sessions.

Basic skills that build a rewarding relationship include learning to listen without interrupting; stating your own thoughts, feelings, and needs; being able to put yourself in her place; sharing information that is interesting or amusing; acknowledging her thoughts, feelings, and point of view; and developing the ability to compromise.

Trust is the foundation of a relationship, but the framework in which you experience that trust is created by the quality of the communication you have with each other.

The following basic points will increase your effectiveness in communication so that you will be understood and in turn understand the other person, and so that both of you will feel comfortable with what is being said.

Don't interrupt. Interrupting often occurs because as one woman speaks, feelings and defensiveness are stimulated in the other. Allowing the first speaker to finish often involves managing discomfort internally. Taking a deep breath may help, as well as allowing adequate time for conversations where there is likely to be conflict between you, so that each of you feels confident that there will be time for you to express yourself.

Use no more than three sentences at a time when discussing something important. Misunderstandings develop if you use more than three sentences about something meaningful, as it is difficult to take in more information than this at one time.

Listen to her thoughts and feelings, instead of planning your next comment. Many people fail to get the other person's message clearly because they are mentally preparing what they are going to say in response. It is often better to check out your impressions of what your partner is saying before you respond. Your response needs to fit her *actual* meaning, not what you assume it to be. When checking out, be direct: "The impression I'm getting is ... Is that correct?"

Avoid starting sentences with *you*; start them with *I*. Say, "I need help with the housework." Do not say, "You're no help around the house."

Say, "I feel angry when you do that." Do not say, "You make me so angry when you do that."

If you start a sentence with *you* it is much more likely that the response you get will be defensive, because she feels attacked or criticized.

Mention what is positive about the other person's comments, before you state where you disagree. She will be much more able to hear your disagreement if she believes you have heard something positive as well.

If she says something that is hurtful to you, assume she has good intentions, unless proven otherwise. Even though her *intentions* are good, her communication style may be hurtful or insensitive.

Kerry and Ione return home from the gym where they have spent some time talking with Kerry's best friend, Zelda. There is tension between them on the walk home.

Ione: How was your workout?
Kerry: Fine.
Ione: What'll we do this afternoon?
Kerry: I don't care.
Ione: Is something wrong?
Kerry: Yeah. You obviously don't care whether we spend time together.
Ione: What are you talking about?

Kerry: The way you invited Zelda along on our date night.

Ione: What do you mean?

Kerry: Friday. We spend Friday nights together. I seem to be the only one that matters to.

Ione: You mean because I talked to Zelda about seeing that movie, and maybe doing it Friday?

Kerry: Of course that's what I mean.

Ione: Honey, I didn't mean to hurt your feelings. I'm really sorry. It never occurred to me. I love Friday nights with you, too. It's just that you've been saying you never get to see Zelda ... and she's so busy. Forgive me?

Kerry needs to mentally give Ione a chance. The attitude, "Ione cares about me. There must be a good reason she is willing to share Friday with Zelda," would save them both unnecessary pain.

Avoid name-calling, sarcasm, mimicking. When these occur, people tend to feel that there is a hostile attack going on. They are likely to counterattack or to become defensive. Both reactions destroy communication.

Avoid using the words *never* and *always*. Whatever you are trying to communicate, once she hears the words *never* or *always* a barrier goes up. Instead of being heard for whatever it is you are trying to communicate, a conflict begins over the sweeping statement you have made. It is much better to use *frequently, often,* or *sometimes*.

If you are discussing an issue or problem that you feel strongly about, the simple statement "This is something that bothers me" can also be effective.

Hearing this, the other person is much less likely to go on the defensive, and much more inclined to listen to what you are communicating.

Try to avoid judgments. If you want something, or you dislike something, it is best just to say "I would prefer" or "It concerns me that..." rather than putting a value judgment forward such as "I think it's awfully stupid that you do..." or "It's really awful when you..."

If you insist on making value judgments, instead of hearing what you are saying, she will respond by feeling defensive, angry, or depressed, and she is likely to withdraw or to escalate the situation into open conflict.

Mention successes. Talking about what works well in a relationship is at least as important as talking about difficulties. Noticing successes validates your relationship and the efforts you make to maintain it. If you identify what made you successful in one area of your relationship, you might be able to use the same style or methods to tackle another challenge.

Faye and Renata are putting away their Christmas decorations. Faye says with a grin, "We really did great this year. Remember how much we fought last Christmas?"

"Yeah," says Renata, "I think it really helped that we talked about how we felt about our families coming, before they got here."

Faye nods. "And your idea about asking your cousin to help us with your mom really worked. Every time your mom started to criticize something, Evelyn just changed the subject."

Velma and Bea are laughing and obviously having

a good time. "Can you believe," says Velma, "that we
had a fight an hour ago, and not only are we speaking again, but we're laughing!"

"Well, you just saw the error of your ways," Bea
teases.

Velma pulls Bea down on their bed. "I used to
feel our relationship was doomed when we fought.
I'm so glad we learned to listen to each other."

When a couple is going through a difficult time,
it's a valuable idea to review successes. It's a way of
saying, "There are things we do well, even though
we're having difficulty right now."

Successes count, whether they require little effort,
such as remembering to call your lover when you're
going to be late because you know it's important to
her, or if they need an extended period of planning
and effort, such as learning to discuss your finances
without fighting or defensiveness.

Large or small, each success is a sign of willingness and effectiveness in keeping your relationship
vital and strong.

Acknowledge each other. Hearing in words the
positive impact you have on each other will create a
sense of warmth and well-being. The positive impact
may come from the way your lover looks, sounds,
smells, feels, thinks, behaves. It may come from what
she believes, how she treats herself, you, or others.
When you acknowledge your lover you need to
include (a) what it is you experience about her, and
(b) the impact the experience has on you.

"When we spend time together, I feel really
good."

"I heard you express your opinion at the meeting last night, and I felt proud to be your partner."

"I appreciated so much that you called my sister to see how she felt after her surgery."

"I felt your support while I was studying for my exams. It really helped me."

"You know how to make our apartment comfortable and beautiful. I'm lucky to live with you."

If each woman in a relationship takes time each day to acknowledge her partner for at least one thing, both women will feel appreciated.

Wait for the right moment. "I'm going to talk to Ann about some things that are bothering me, but we've both been busy, and this week she's having her period," says Marguerite. She will wait for a time when it will feel right to talk about a topic uncomfortable for both of them.

There are times that are unwise or inconsiderate to bring up angry feelings or potentially upsetting topics. It is safe to predict that discussions of a problem will not go smoothly if one or both of you are exhausted or seriously ill, have recently experienced a death, are threatened with losing your job, or if you are already angry about other things in your life. These and other worries will inevitably present serious impediments to a successful discussion.

It is, however, unwise to expect that good timing will eliminate the discomfort that comes with a difficult topic, although it may make it a little easier to introduce the subject into conversation. It is best if you are both rested and there is adequate time to complete your discussion. Be direct, and let her know that you need to have a talk about a particular issue. It is better not to postpone it too long, because the sooner you bring up a topic that is bothering you, the less likely it is that it will grow to explosive proportions.

Use conversational flags to initiate uncomfortable topics. On a beach, colored flags communicate information — blue for calm waters, green for choppy, and red for dangerous currents.

Conversational flags can similarly signal that the topic coming up may be upsetting.

Jennifer and Elena are skilled at posting flags. Jennifer leaves Elena a message on her answering machine: "I've got some stuff to talk about. Nothing heavy, though."

On another occasion she alerts Elena to prepare herself to listen in as relaxed and nondefensive a manner as possible with this message: "Honey, I've got something to tell you that might be hard to hear. Is this an okay time for me to do it?"

A red flag is only posted to signal extremely serious matters such as an imminent breakup, legal or financial crises, suspicion about affairs, serious medical conditions. There needs to be no doubt that a red flag topic is about to be introduced: "Jennifer, we have something really serious to talk about. I'm going to cancel my plans for the evening, can you?"

3. Managing or Eliminating Serious Problems

There is no such person as a problem-free partner. Some problems, however, are more likely to damage a loving relationship than others. If you yourself are struggling with such a problem, or if you love someone who is, you can either work toward resolution before starting a relationship or you can plan ahead to eliminate, or at least manage, the problem while you are in the relationship.

Expect that, at best, these serious issues will strain your relationship. Without effective action, the damage will very likely be irreversible.

Problems most likely to erode loving feelings include substance abuse; clinical depression; financial irresponsibility; untreated physical or emotional illness; incomplete separation from parents; childhood abuse; unfinished feelings about a past lover; conflictual relationship with past partner with whom you are coparenting children; low self-esteem; unclear sense of your feelings, beliefs, or direction in life; and dishonesty.

Information and resources to cope with these problems are abundant. Here are initial contacts that are helpful. These contacts may be the source of a solution or may lead to additional resources.

Substance abuse. Alcoholics Anonymous, Overeaters Anonymous, and Narcotics Anonymous are well-established, highly responsive organizations with an established success rate. Consult your telephone directory. Expect to be given information about meetings and possibly a contact person to support you for an initial meeting. Your physician or nurse practitioner can also be useful as an initial contact.

Clinical depression. Should you experience several of the following, it is possible you have an illness — clinical depression: Your energy is low, no matter how much you sleep; your appetite has significantly increased or decreased; you are irritable; you have less interest in sex; you feel sad often; your motivation and zest for life have decreased; you think a lot about your faults and past mistakes; you would like your life to be over.

If you think you may have clinical depression, consult an internist, gynecologist, nurse practitioner, psychiatrist, or psychopharmacologist. Expect to answer questions about your history and your family's history of depressive symptoms. You may be given a questionnaire to fill out. Expect to discuss the possibility of medication or therapy. Expect to be encouraged to exercise and to reduce your intake of alcohol and sugars.

Financial irresponsibility. You need to identify the main cause of your difficulty. You may lack information or skills, you may be coping with an emotional problem, or you may have a compulsion. The first step is to assess the problem with an objective person or persons. Perhaps you might consult a therapist to sort out the problem. A plan to change your financial situation could include consultation with a vocational counselor, bankruptcy attorney, or financial planner, or a referral to Debtors Anonymous. Your local bookstore should have a section on finances and money management that would include books with practical guidance.

Untreated physical or emotional illness. The solution is twofold: (a) initiate a plan for taking care of your difficulty, and (b) understand why you have neglected to take care of yourself.

It is important to select one health-care provider you can trust to be the overall manager of your care. Referrals may be available at the gay and lesbian community center nearest you. Avoidance of self-care usually has an emotional or financial component. If your finances are a barrier to care, thoroughly search your community for resources. Call your county health department, seek out women's health centers, contact the state mental health department, or call the state psychological association and inquire about doctors and therapists who operate on a sliding scale or low-fee basis. If you can afford health care but avoid it, consult a therapist to sort out the reasons that prevent you from taking good care of yourself.

Incomplete separation from parents. Becoming independent of one's parents involves a set of practical and emotional experiences that must come before a person establishes an adult relationship. If your feelings about your parents and your parents' feelings about you are issues in your daily life or in your relationship, consider consulting a therapist to complete the emotional work of becoming a woman separate from, though still caring about, your parents.

Childhood abuse. *The Courage to Heal* by Ellen Bass and Laura Davis is an excellent resource. For many women a combination of work with an individual counselor and group meetings or workshops can be highly effective. If you are in a relationship, it is essential that your partner become involved in a support group while you are going through this intense process.

Unfinished feelings about a past lover. An active process to finish feelings for a past lover is described in the section headed Finishing Relationships in Chapter 10, "Lessons Learned from Past Relationships."

Conflictual relationship with past partner

with whom you are coparenting. Primarily for the child or children involved, but also for yourself and your current partner, seek joint therapy and possibly mediation with your past partner. If she is reluctant, ask family or friends whom you know she respects to intervene. Your pediatrician, local gay and lesbian community service center, and your religious or spiritual guide may be helpful with a referral. Seek a therapist with a family-systems background. If your partner will not go, go alone. Perhaps she will eventually join you, but in the meantime you are gaining the skills and insights to cope with the situation.

Low self-esteem. Consult your local bookstore for books and workbooks on the subject of low self-esteem. Counseling, therapy, and self-esteem workshops are helpful remedies. Do a self-assessment on whether or not you are living up to your potential, then make a detailed plan to change. Your plan should include goals and specific actions with time frames to achieve these goals.

Shame has a particularly damaging effect on self-esteem. Women are taught to be ashamed of their bodies, their aggression, their sexuality, their ambition, their feelings. Women are taught to feel ashamed when they are molested, raped, beaten, and abused. Women are taught to be ashamed of poverty, wealth, confidence, and lack of confidence. Shame erodes self-esteem and dictates secrecy about all that is shameful.

During the last twenty years lesbians have been part of a variety of women's experiences that counteract shame with knowledge and acceptance. Lesbians have been bringing to light their previously hidden life experiences. Consciousness-raising groups, workshops, friendship groups, and discussions with spiritual leaders and therapists have proven effective in letting go of shame, expressing anger, and increasing self-esteem.

One such experience occurs in Apache Junction, Arizona, where women meet on Sunday evenings for potluck and the sharing of herstory. Each week one woman tells the story of her life, often by focusing on one theme, such as losses, oppression, successes.

In a 1996 interview, Shevy Healy, Ph.D., organizer of OLAC — Old Lesbians Organizing for Change — said, "a feeling of safety exists in the group that allows the women to share openly things they have never revealed before."

It is powerful to be able to state: "This is who I am, and this is what I have experienced."

Unclear sense of your feelings, beliefs, or direction in life. If you have an unclear sense of your feelings, beliefs, or direction in life, start by keeping a journal, if possible every day, in which you record your personal observations and any reactions of which you are aware. Record your feelings and frustrations. Make a wish list of experiences you would like to have in life. These could be related to work, recreation, or personal development. Write about what you think keeps you from embracing your wishes.

A session with a therapist can be helpful in selecting which techniques might help you gain greater clarity. The therapist might suggest a course of therapy. It is appropriate to ask what could be gained and how long it might take. The therapist might also refer you to classes, workshops, or readings.

A consultation with a vocational counselor would include talking, testing, and having a report compiled based on the tests. Job categories that are appropriate to your interests and skills would be identified.

Dishonesty. If dishonesty is a problem you have, it will interfere with all aspects of your life and relationship and may ultimately negatively affect your health. Consult a therapist. Expect that you will not be judged but will be helped to understand the source of your dishonesty and be helped to make a plan to change. Seek guidance from a spiritual or religious leader. Expect to be encouraged and strengthened.

4. Extending Beyond One's Own Comfort Zone

Some differences between two in a relationship are inevitable. These differences will lead to requests that you share experiences and be with people that on your own you would not consider.

You do not have to merge and become your partner. Maintaining your individuality is important to you and stimulating to her. An openness to experiences she prefers will create a sense of sharing and will make her feel valued.

Each woman must state clearly which experiences are important to be shared, for example:

"It would mean a lot to me if you'd come to the

office picnic. I know they might talk about work too much, but they're really nice and I'd like to show you off."

"I know you feel self-conscious dancing, but is there anything we can do? take a class? dance at home? It really is my favorite thing to do."

"I love our vacation at your cousin's cabin every summer. But Angela and Liz are organizing a river rafting trip this year. Let's at least hear more about it before you say no."

"I'm very turned on and I've always wanted you to make love to me outside. No one can see into our backyard and I love looking up at the big tree. What do you say?"

5. Maintaining Perspective

Strain on a relationship is reduced when both women can maintain a sense of what is important to react to and what isn't. If a basic assumption can be made that both people care and are well intentioned, then many instances of inattentiveness, small slights, and minor hurts can be viewed as the ordinary predictable experiences of two human beings relating to each other. It is difficult to maintain a sense of loving and being loved if small missteps lead to fighting and other strong emotional responses that have to be analyzed, explained, and accounted for.

On the other hand, serious issues must be commented on and addressed, otherwise an erosion of the relationship occurs.

Some questions to ask to gain perspective are:

- Is the issue at hand a threat to health or safety?
- Is what's bothering me a one-time occurrence, or is it something that happens frequently?
- How strongly do I feel about this issue?
- Am I keeping a sense of the relationship as a whole while I am concerned about the current problem?
- Could I be overreacting because of fatigue, illness, or other stress in my life?
- Could I be overreacting because this experience reminds me of other experiences in my past?

6. Creating and Using Adequate Support

Your support group is made up of people who believe in the best parts of you and who see and accept the parts of you that need improvement.

Because no two people can meet all of each other's needs, supportive people either fill in what is missing in a relationship or expand and increase what is already there.

Support does not eliminate the need for skill and commitment on the part of a loving couple. However, it is often mentioned as the factor that made the crucial difference in maintaining a relationship through the many difficult phases life brings.

A support group is like a life jacket worn while sailing. You may never actually use it, but if the waters get rough you feel more secure, and if you fall overboard you have a much better chance of survival.

Use the following questionnaire to see how well supported your relationship is.

How Much Support Does
My Relationship Have?

	YES	NO
1. I have at least one close friend that I talk with on a regular basis. One of the things we talk about is my relationship.	☐	☐
2. I have at least one close friend who lets me know my relationship is good for me.	☐	☐
3. I have at least one person in my life who encourages me to work on my relationship when I complain about it.	☐	☐
4. I have at least one person in my life who confronts me about ways I could improve myself.	☐	☐
5. I talk with at least one person who is known to be successful in personal relationships.	☐	☐
6. My partner and I socialize with other couples.	☐	☐
7. My partner and I learn some ways to manage our relationship from watching or talking with other couples.	☐	☐
8. We know at least two other people in a relationship who both work at making their relationship satisfying to them.	☐	☐
9. We belong to a spiritual or religious group that is supportive of our relationship.	☐	☐
10. We attend community activities where we are recognized as a couple.	☐	☐
11. At least one member of our families acknowledges our relationship.	☐	☐

12. We are accepted as a couple by one or both
    of our families.   □   □
13. We socialize as a couple with members of our
    families.   □   □
14. If we were in a relationship crisis, at least
    one member of our families would encourage
    us to work it out.   □   □
15. We have learned useful information from
    observing how the couples in our families
    work.   □   □
16. If my partner and I were facing a problem
    today, we know at least one person to talk
    with who we believe would be helpful.   □   □
17. If my partner and I were celebrating a
    special event in our relationship, we have
    people with whom to share it.   □   □
18. If our relationship was in crisis, we know a
    professional counselor, religious leader, or
    therapist we would be willing to consult.   □   □
19. If either of us were seriously ill, we know
    we have people who would help us during
    the illness.   □   □
20. If we were facing a financial crisis, we have
    people we could ask for help.   □   □

KEY Add the number of *yes* answers to find the level of your support.

16–20 Your relationship is well supported. Can you learn anything from your *no* answers?

11–15 You have enough support to maintain your relationship. You would feel more comfortable and problem-solve more readily if you raised your *yes* score.

6–10 You have enough support to manage when your life and relationship are running smoothly. You have less support than you need for the rough times. Have a conversation about your *no* answers. Some sources of support are outside of your control, but perhaps you and your partner can make a plan to begin increasing the supports which you can influence.

0–5 You are too isolated and rely too heavily on each other. If you are maintaining your relationship now with this level of support, there could be difficulties ahead. Developing a support group is wise preparation. Talk seriously about both your willingness and your reluctance to increase your supports. The process of reaching out will enrich your life.

7. Dealing with Conflict Constructively

Most couples fight. There are ways to handle conflict that do not damage the loving quality of a relationship.

Fighting dissipates tension. The sooner you recognize that tension is building and take corrective action, the less intense the fighting will be.

Weapons deemed too destructive for military action are banned by international treaty. A similar ban is essential in relationships. Behaviors that need to be off-limits in a fight are

- Intentionally inflicting pain
- Threatening a person's sense of safety
- Degrading each other
- One person making the other "wrong"

- One woman attacking the other with personal information that has been previously shared
- Any physical attack

Without exception, the preceding behaviors should be banned between you because they are so destructive.

Some fighting styles prolong fights or make them ugly. It is important to remember that any love, however strong initially, can be eroded. The following can corrode and eventually destroy love:

- Name calling
- Questioning the other partner's character
- Screaming or shouting
- Mentioning that other people also see her in a negative light
- Threatening to leave or end the relationship
- Telling the other person to leave or end the relationship
- Using biting sarcasm
- Belittling
- Comparing the other to someone she dislikes

Some fighting styles are not particularly harmful but are ineffective. These include

- Fighting about more than one topic at a time
- Bringing up examples from the past that neither of you can do anything about now

- Refusing to continue talking when the two of you haven't reached any resolution
- Minimizing or exaggerating complaints
- Failing to take responsibility for your part of the problem
- Stomping away or slamming doors
- Talking about each other rather than talking about the problem

There may not be such a thing as a "good fight," but if you and your partner want to handle conflict effectively, you could both expect to

- Make direct statements that include emotions, such as, "I'm so angry with you for forgetting to pick up the cleaning again. I really needed my blue jacket for work tomorrow."
- Listen without interrupting
- Tolerate raised voices and angry tones
- Hear some criticism as long as it isn't framed as a put-down
- Tolerate some tension without panicking, attacking, or leaving
- Hear examples of what is annoying the other person
- Respond without automatically defending oneself
- Acknowledge each person's part in the problem
- Feel that things have been resolved when each of you has expressed your emotions,

defined the problem, and looked at possible
solutions together
• Apologize for any violations of fair fighting

There is no "normal" amount of fighting for any
one couple. When couples problem-solve, most will
experience some annoyance and irritation that occasionally reaches the level of a fight. However, if you
find there is frequent conflict between you, there
could be several possible reasons.

• You are very different from each other and
  need to accept your differences
• You have unrealistic expectations of each
  other
• You need to recognize that you are frustrated before you reach the level of fighting
• You need to increase your problem-solving
  skills
• You are repeating a pattern you saw in
  childhood
• There is sexual tension in the relationship
• One or both of you experience increased ir-
  ritability with hormonal changes
• You need to evaluate your use of alcohol
  or drugs
• One partner is depressed (it may be both)
• Your stress level is high, and you need to
  adopt stress management techniques such
  as exercise, deep relaxation, or therapy
• You are basically incompatible

If intense, angry emotion lasts more than five
minutes, it is wise to take a break from each other

to cool down. The time-out can be used to breathe deeply, take a walk, write in a journal, think through what is frustrating you, call a friend/sponsor/therapist, or express your anger out loud alone, where your words can do no damage.

Couples who are reluctant to take a time-out and continue fighting at high intensity levels are very likely damaging their relationship and need to consider the following

- Some people are afraid of closeness and fight to prevent it
- Some people are addicted to intense experiences and fight to get an "intensity fix"
- Some people come from abusive backgrounds and need therapy to work out the effects of the abuse
- Some people have serious difficulty with impulse control and need therapy to learn how to do it

In order to set ground rules for your fights, you need to be able to tell your partner what words or topics are off limits. Consider if any of the following would be very painful for you:

- Being called names, such as *bitch, brat, princess, geek,* or any other term you find personally insulting
- Having your intelligence or mental health attacked with statements such as "You're stupid" or "You're crazy"
- Threats to end the relationship
- Threats to leave

- Being compared to other people, such as
  her past lovers, your mother, or someone
  else — "You're just like . . ."
- Sarcasm
- Angry comments intended to stop
  discussion, such as, "Shut up" or "Fuck off"
- Telling you negative things others have
  said about you
- Other unacceptable comments that "push
  your hot button"

Have a conversation with your lover about what
her off-limits list would be. You can then both make
an honest effort to avoid what is exceptionally painful
during a fight. If you cross a line, apologize.

Emotional bloodbaths are destructive for both the
person and the relationship. Learning to resolve conflict constructively adds to the loving quality of your
relationship.

Additional Steps

Preserving love is a dynamic process that requires
each woman's ongoing commitment and involvement.
Two further steps would be to spend quiet time alone
and to spend time with other couples.

Spend quiet time alone. Spend some quiet time
alone every week. Without the distraction of other
people or intense activity, there is an opportunity for

intimate sharing. Be natural during these times and let talking, quiet, sharing, or sex evolve.

Spend time with other couples. Spend time with other couples whose relationships you admire. Other couples — gay, lesbian, or straight — are a valuable resource. Ask them what has helped them be close, and what keeps their relationship alive.

Chapter 7:

Enhancing Love

Couples talk about deepening of their relationship. Others mention honeymoon times after being together many years. How do these experiences come about? If you have a good relationship now, it is possible to enhance the love and closeness you already have, to build on that foundation an even deeper and more rewarding union.

The following checklist will help couples who have been relating to each other for more than a year assess the overall relationship.

Relationship Satisfaction Checklist
Each person answers *yes, no,* or *sometimes.*

	YES	NO	SOME-TIMES
1. Overall I feel very satisfied with our relationship.	☐	☐	☐
2. I think we communicate well.	☐	☐	☐
3. I think we handle conflict well.	☐	☐	☐
4. I like the way we express affection.	☐	☐	☐
5. I feel loved.	☐	☐	☐
6. I feel loving.	☐	☐	☐
7. We are respectful of each other.	☐	☐	☐
8. We have a mutually satisfying sex life.	☐	☐	☐
9. We handle finances well.	☐	☐	☐
10. We trust each other.	☐	☐	☐
11. We enjoy each other's company.	☐	☐	☐
12. We can count on each other in times of trouble.	☐	☐	☐
13. We both enjoy relationships with other people.	☐	☐	☐
14. We bring out the best in each other.	☐	☐	☐
15. We help each other develop our potential.	☐	☐	☐
16. Our relationship endures regardless of changes in us and changes in our lives.	☐	☐	☐
17. We have (a) satisfactory living situation(s).	☐	☐	☐
18. We take vacations together.	☐	☐	☐
19. We respect each other's values.	☐	☐	☐

20. Additional reasons we think we have a good relationship:

KEY Give yourself 1 point for each *yes* answer

and one point for each additional reason you listed in Number 20.

15 points or more: You have a very satisfying relationship at this time.

You can have useful discussions about the questions you and your partner answered differently, or for those you agreed were *no* or *sometimes*. Ask each other how important the issues in each question are and whether or not either of you would want to make changes.

Bear in mind there are no completely flawless relationships, and trying to be perfect causes more tension than realistically looking for improvement.

Ways to Deepen a Relationship

Share significant life experiences. Life inevitably presents us with many opportunities to deepen a relationship: illness, crisis, deaths and other losses, national and local disasters, financial reverses or gains, successes and promotions, and significant passages, such as births, graduations, anniversary celebrations, and commitment ceremonies.

Enter into each of these experiences as fully as you can with each other. Open your hearts and share your time and your feelings. Put these significant life experiences high on your personal priority list so that work or other commitments do not prevent you from experiencing them fully.

If you find that either of you avoids participation in significant life experiences, try to gain an understanding of your reluctance. Don't deceive yourself about the importance of sharing the joys and sadnesses of life. If you are hesitant, ask yourself what your family demonstrated about sharing the facts, feelings, and mutual experiencing of life events.

If you have friends who are able to embrace life on an emotional level, talk with them about your reluctance. If you are afraid or uncomfortable with the feelings that these significant events evoke, seek therapy to ease your fears.

Through sharing a great deal is gained — an emotional bonding, the building of a mutual history, joy, a sense that you can count on each other, and an overall deepening of the relationship.

Courageously share who you are. We are dynamic beings, and if we practice self-awareness, we know that we have ever-changing thoughts, feelings, and experiences to share. You give your partner the opportunity to love you more deeply when you share the complex, sometimes confusing, often irrational workings of your inner world. It creates a deeper relationship if you know all of someone and are still able to love her and if she knows you in the same way.

Learn to give. Learn to give to your partner what she wants and needs, not just what you enjoy giving.

Brittany is an outgoing, warm woman who is known for organizing wonderful parties. You can hear her laughter as she moves from group to group of guests. During their first year of living together, Brittany gave Eleanor a surprise birthday party. Sixty people attended, and everyone said it was one of the best parties they had ever experienced. Eleanor appreciated Brittany's generosity and the attention of their friends.

By the third year of their relationship, however, Brittany realized that it was *she* who enjoyed parties, not Eleanor. What made Eleanor feel loved and special was time alone with Brittany, or spending an evening talking with another couple. When Brittany suggested these activities, it made Eleanor feel more understood and more deeply loved.

Share laughter and fun. It is well documented that laughter not only adds to the pleasure of life but also increases one's sense of health and well-being.

Humor breaks tension, helping you look at issues from an different angle and thus changing the whole feeling and tone of the situation. Humor is an essential coping tool — if you can't laugh, life becomes unbearable.

A person who can access the playful side of herself, and at times look at life as a child does, is able to find and share humor in life's activities, and enrich her partner's life. Jane says, "Not only will Trudie face the serious things of life with me, she's so much fun, she makes me laugh."

Participate in couples workshops or couples therapy. It isn't necessary to have a problem in your relationship to benefit from a workshop or a discussion with a therapist. Exercises in workshops or the observations of a therapist will often expand your own view or bring to light issues that may be limiting your involvement with each other.

The Benefits of Differences

When you develop a relationship, you become aware of differences and learn not to personalize them. It is possible to use differences to your benefit in an established relationship.

Stimulation. A partner who is different from you can introduce you to new worlds and new experiences, providing you with an opportunity to view people and life in a way you could not do on your own.

Personal growth. You will be challenged to examine your personal style and point of view when you interact with someone different. A sense of sameness can make us feel secure, but it can also become stale. The questioning of a mind that operates differently from our own may be temporarily irritating, but then it opens doors in our own thoughts and feelings, creating a sense of expansion.

Complementary skills. If each of you has abilities the other does not, the challenge is to appreciate what each partner brings that enriches the relationship. Any sense of competition or inadequacy can be transformed into an appreciation that more is available within the relationship.

Dee explains that when she and Colleen started living together they were always fighting. Dee says, "We think about things differently. I'm intuitive and Colleen's analytical. We drove each other bonkers until we realized we've got two great minds here. Let's use them both."

Charlotte and Rachel were concerned about having enough time together because of their differences. Mildred says, "I'm a people person who fell in love with a computer geek. We weren't sure how this was going to work out. Five years ago we started a business. I'm out front with the customers. Charlotte has us so organized it's amazing. We're together a lot, yet we can do our own thing."

Don't fight your differences. Explore how you can use them in your whole relationship.

Honeymoon Times

The early feelings of I-can't-wait excitement and passion change as your partner becomes more real to you. However, many couples find that the honeymoon feelings can return throughout life. They are the special times of high energy in the relationship. Sometimes a honeymoon spontaneously appears. Following are some ways to increase the probability that you will have these peak experiences.

Live your life in a way that allows you to reach your potential as much as possible. This refers to your work life as well as to your interests, your physical well-being, your relationships, your spirituality. Feeling the excitement and satisfaction that comes from times of growth is often the fuel for a time of high emotional or sexual energy. Working toward your potential, both as an individual and as a couple, can be an ongoing undertaking.

Experience what is positive about yourself, your life, and your partner. In the beginning of your relationship it's likely all you were able to see were the positives as you effortlessly floated on the captivating feeling that all was right with the world.

Now that time has given you a deeper understanding of your relationship, you can continue to have the opportunity to respond to positives that are now woven into a more complex view of each other. The key is focusing, as your emotions will respond to whatever your attention is fixed upon.

Jami and Adele have lived together for five years. They are raising their son, Paul, whom Jami adopted, and their daughter, Liana, of whom Adele was the birth mother.

Jami says, "I was crazy about Adele when we met, and I thought we'd have this great family and be happy most of the time. The truth is, it's really hard. We get so involved with the kids — Paul has epilepsy and Liana had colic for six months. My mom had a stroke and lived with us for almost a year. It was getting to be too much, and we were fighting.

"We finally figured out we have to count our blessings. We're teaching the kids too. Every night at dinner we say one thing we appreciate about one another, and one good thing that happened during the day."

Francine explains how disappointment affected her relationship with Hilda. "Hilda is beautiful and very warm. She always makes me laugh. But, of course, she isn't perfect. Whenever she would annoy me, I would get so disappointed, as if she was spoiling my picture of our relationship, and I would think about what she had done and get more and more upset, until all I could see was what was wrong with her and us.

"We talked with my cousin, who has a really good outlook on life. She's helped me to hold on to all that is good about Hilda and us, even when Hilda really annoys me."

Try something new together. A first-time experience generates curiosity and a sense of vitality. Try something new. Hike a different trail or bike a new path; attend a lecture by a spiritual leader outside your faith; paint your bedroom an adventuresome color; actively make new friends; create a recipe together. Newness is what enchanted you on the first honeymoon and can stimulate you now.

Be honest with yourself about your selfishness in the relationship. We are all somewhat selfish. You are probably aware right now of one or two things that would make your partner feel special that you could do more generously. On the first honeymoon you would have done anything for each other, and you remember how each of you responded then.

Interact with people who are passionate about life. There are people who are passionate about their lives and their relationships. Such people are vital — they *care*. Other people's passion can inspire our own.

Expose yourself to challenges. Be open to conversations, books, music, movies, plays, and art that stir you, upset you, challenge you. This stimulation helps you stay open. Openness is crucial to forging a deep, rewarding relationship.

If sex is part of your relationship, embrace opportunities to be sexual. If the thought of making love goes through your mind, if you feel turned on by a movie or book, take action. The spontaneity of these moments makes a relationship feel fresh. Don't let fatigue or something nonessential that is already planned stop the expression of your sexuality.

Go away together. Find a way each year to spend time away from your usual routine. Elaborate vacations are not necessary — *change* is.

Enhancing your relationship means that you go *deeper,* so that you:

- Know each other fully
- Share experiences that have high emotional impact
- Keep growing, together and individually
- Use differences to your mutual advantage
- Share laughter and fun

Chapter 8:

The Problem of Ex-Lovers

Many lesbians prefer to continue friendships with ex-lovers. Friendship was a significant part of their relationship and they choose not to lose the sharing, the history, and the experience of being known well after the relationship itself is over.

Because lesbian communities are small, exes are more likely to continue to be part of one's social group than in the majority culture.

There are positive and negative aspects of life with exes that will affect you as an individual and also affect your subsequent relationships.

Gilda plays tennis twice a week with her ex and

goes on skiing vacations with her. They continue to
jointly own a mountain cabin. Gilda is clear that she
is now in love with Maria and simply enjoys a friendship with her ex. However, the relationship is a
source of great friction between Gilda and Maria,
since Maria doesn't feel secure with the situation.

Lei is grateful that Maile is friends with her ex,
Stephanie. When Maile complains about Lei,
Stephanie confronts Maile about her part in the problem. "I know how you are. You were the same way
with me."

Nadia works with her ex, Summer, and Summer's
new lover, Yvette. Summer wants them all to be
friends, and Nadia puts on a good act, but her work
life is now painful. She feels hurt and rejected when
Summer pays attention to Yvette.

Wendy had wanted to break up with Felice one
year into their two-and-a-half-year relationship, but
they are partners in a performing country-western
dance group. Wendy worried that she would have to
give up the dancing, which has enriched her life. She
was relieved when she and Felice broke up but
remained friends and dance partners. They now have
a strong four-way friendship with their new lovers,
who are supportive of the dancing Felice and Wendy
do together.

These couples illustrate the variety of forms relationships with ex-lovers may take and show that you
always need to consider the impact on your future

life when you are deciding what role you want your ex to play.

There are commonly three phases in the transformation from lover to ex-lover. Each phase presents challenges to the former partners. Managing these challenges determines the amount of pain each woman feels and the amount of negative emotion that will persist once the two separate.

Phase One: Immediately Following the Breakup

During this time four difficult issues usually emerge: handling your anger toward each other; providing information to, and spending time with, people you shared; dividing joint property; and making arrangements to continue contact with children or pets you have cared for jointly.

In an ideal world, you would have discussed these four items at the beginning of your relationship so that you have a plan in place should a separation occur in the future.

Anger

Anger is a natural reaction to the hurt and rejection of a breakup. It also comes from the frustration of a relationship not working out, of time wasted, and from whatever complaints and disappointments you each have. If dishonesty is part of the breakup, there is another possible level of anger — rage.

Some people value their anger because it lessens an awareness of feelings of grief and helplessness.

There are some constructive ways that couples can work out their anger during a breakup:

- Talk to friends and family about your anger. Select people who are good listeners, who can be supportive, and who will remind you that you had a part in the breakup.
- Write in a journal about your anger, hurt, and loss.
- Agree to exchange letters in which you express your anger. Try to acknowledge your part in what has angered your partner by return letter.
- Agree to listen to each other's anger for a set period of time. For example, you might meet for forty minutes and take turns sharing and listening in ten-minute intervals. Ground rules must be set. The person who is listening may not interrupt and may not defend herself. The person who is sharing may not name-call or demean. At the end of the time period, each person must sincerely try to express regret for the pain her behavior caused, even if she did not mean to cause pain. Most couples find this process difficult without a mediator. You could try it on your own or ask an objective person to facilitate the process.
- Go to therapy as a couple to express your

anger to each other with a third person
giving guidance.

- Go to therapy alone to release your anger
  and gain a better understanding of the
  relationship.
- Talk with a religious or spiritual counselor
  to express your feelings and gain a new
  perspective.
- Work toward an acceptance that everyone
  has flaws and limitations.
- Participate in physical activity that releases
  aggression, such as brisk walking, running,
  pounding on a mattress or pillow, hitting a
  punching bag, playing tennis or racquetball.

Beneath the anger that erupts with the loss of a
lover is a layer of softer, and often raw, emotions.
These include hurt, sadness, disappointment, vulnerability, helplessness, and rejection. Feeling a deep ache,
needing to cry, and needing comfort are natural when
you deal with these deep feelings. Although it is
sometimes possible, it is complicated for the couple
breaking up to share these emotions and to do so
with a genuine caring for each other's pain.

Women comment on the difficulties of sharing
hurt by saying things like, "I'm used to getting comfort from her when I'm sad, but she is making me
sad, so how can I let her comfort me?" "I don't want
to let her see how much she's hurt me." "I'm too
angry at her to cry with her." "She says she's sad
we're over, but it was her choice to end it, so I can't
exactly feel sympathy for her."

For these reasons, more women share their sadness and pain with supportive friends, family, a

therapist, or sponsor. The most important thing to remember is that sadness is a part of ending and that it needs to be expressed. Held inside, it can create physical problems or a barrier in your next relationship.

Gloria reports that her doctor referred her to a therapist when no physical basis for her headaches was discovered. "I went through a breakup eight months ago. I got really mad and then got on with my life. I believe that when something is over, it's over. The therapist told me I needed to cry and talk about what I missed and what I had valued about the relationship. I didn't believe her, and I didn't like the idea. She had me write my feelings in a journal and talk out loud to my ex as if she were in the room. I was surprised how much I cried. I felt a lot better."

Couples who do choose to share the sadness and pain of their breakup with each other, need to keep the following points in mind:

- No matter who initiates the breakup for whatever reason, both people go through a loss, and both people feel some pain.
- Ending stimulates a wide variety of emotions, and specific feelings such as relief or anger do not cancel out other feelings such as sadness or hurt.
- However painful the breakup, the good feelings and good experiences were real. Grief is partly about what was once good and is now gone.
- The person initiating the breakup is entitled to her feelings. If you are the

person ending the relationship, guilt or
sorrow about your partner's pain does not
eliminate your own.
- Both people can feel relieved if they can
cry and talk about what the ending means
to each person.
- Talking about pain should not be a source
of blame or punishment but rather a
source of shared human experience.
- It is respectful of the relationship you once
shared to acknowledge its ending, much as
you celebrated its beginning.

People You Have Shared

The breakup of a couple impacts upon all the singles
and couples around them. There is often a recon-
figuring of the social group, based on who remains
friends with whom.

In order to handle joint friends in a loving way,
the couple who are breaking up need to have a
shared view of the reason for the breakup. Talking
through the situation honestly with each other and
sharing information reduces the potential for your
friends taking sides, spreading rumors, and theorizing
about your lives. If the two of you are unclear about
the reasons for the breakup or are unwilling to be
honest with each other or your friends, there will be
more tremors in your friendship group.

Ideally, each needs to be nonpossessive of joint
friends, regardless of who knew the friend prior to
the relationship. Friends are a valuable source of sup-

port during a breakup and may be able to understand both points of view.

Friends and family also need time and opportunity to express their feelings about the situation. They may be sad, threatened, and angry about the loss it creates in their lives.

If dishonesty occurs, such as a new relationship that started prior to the breakup, or the two women don't state the actual reasons for the breakup, the friends you've had in common are more likely to become polarized.

Some ex-couples expect their joint friends to choose sides and express their loyalty by who gets invited to future social events. This right/wrong view of a breakup ignores the important point that both women contribute to the fact that the relationship didn't work. Putting friends in the uncomfortable position of taking sides can alienate them from one or both of you.

Greater stability can be maintained in the lesbian community if friends continue to relate to both people in an ex-couple. When an invitation is issued, the exes can decide if they have worked through their feelings enough for both to attend.

Having a common view of the breakup is the essential point in dealing with joint friends lovingly. A common view can be reached by talking with each other honestly. Protecting your ex from the truth may seem like a caring thing to do, but it is more likely an unwillingness on your part to deal with her pain.

The main reasons it is important for women to talk honestly about a breakup are (a) speaking the truth reinforces the reality of what has happened, thus validating our own sense of what is true, and (b) every time we lie, we move ourselves farther from reality.

Some women believe that they are preventing hurt by not telling the whole truth to ex-partners. In this situation, the woman who is not being told the truth feels off balance, knowing that something is missing.

In an honest talk, both people must take responsibility for their share in the breakup. If it is too difficult to talk honestly alone, a counselor, therapist, objective friend or relative, or spiritual leader could be involved.

While in the short run it may feel powerful to blame oneself or blame the other, there is greater long-term gain in seeing clearly the part each person played and sharing this more complex and accurate view with joint friends.

Dividing Joint Property

Anger and hurt are often expressed in the way that property is divided. In order to handle material items in the most loving way, it is wise to create a written agreement, preferably with an attorney, at the beginning of a committed relationship. If an agreement is not in place, following are some techniques that can help.

- Be clear with yourself about how hurt and wronged you feel. If these feelings are unconscious, they could lead to a sense of unwarranted justification about keeping material things.

- Be clear with yourself about how much you
  want to hurt your ex. Your negotiations
  with her could become a method to inflict
  pain. Ask yourself if you enjoy the idea of
  getting revenge or if you have fantasies of
  getting even in some way.
- Try to be sensitive with each other in
  terms of each person's emotional
  attachment to your joint possessions. If you
  bought the salad bowl but she loves it
  dearly, consider her feelings.
- Create a sense of fairness about how much
  money, time, and effort you each contributed during the relationship. Check
  your impressions with someone objective,
  not someone who will automatically agree
  with you.
- Independently write out what each of you
  would consider a fair and sensitive division
  of property. Read each other's lists before
  discussing them.
- Employ a mediator or attorney who will
  think clearly and fairly.
- Talk with a religious leader or therapist to
  separate the emotional issues from the material things.

Continuing Contact with Children or Pets

Loss of significant adults is emotionally devastating to
children. It is well documented that adults who as
children lose parents, coparents or stepparents will

have difficulty with commitment in adult relationships.

No issue is more important in a breakup than ensuring predictable continuing contact for the child with both members of a couple. For this reason it is important that a couple have a serious commitment before they share their children with each other.

Whatever conflicts arise during a breakup, they should be discussed away from the child and should in no way affect the child's access to both adults.

Deep emotional bonds can be forged with animals, and the feelings of both the pet and the people involved need to be considered at the time of a breakup. Animals are capable of grief, and if the animal's mood changes after a separation, he or she may need contact with your ex.

Phase Two: New Relationships

In the second phase of transitioning from lover to ex, there are two tasks: facing new relationships in each other's lives; and defining what your relationship will now be.

It is never easy to be replaced. Even if you were the person initiating the breakup, expect to react emotionally when your ex is dating and when she forms a new relationship. You will know that you are continuing to resolve your feelings about the breakup if you trash the people she is seeing, if you are happy when she is alone, or if you compare yourself to someone she is seeing. If you once loved her, it is possible to get to the point of wishing her well.

During this time an ex-couple usually think, feel,

and talk about whether to remain friends. This decision affects the ex-couple, their friends and families, and their future partners.

How to Remain Friends

If you want to remain friends, here is a four-step process to transition in a loving way.

1. Be honest with yourself about your motive(s) in wanting to remain friends.

- We were friends before we were lovers
- I'm still in love with her
- I'm hoping we'll get back together
- I want to influence her concerning our property settlement
- I think it's best because we coparent children
- We share an interest in activities we both enjoy
- I enjoy her company but am no longer sexually attracted
- I genuinely like her
- I'm afraid to let go
- She's an important part of my history
- Other . . .

2. Be honest with yourself about the impact exes have had on your relationships in the past.

- No significant impact
- Source of jealousy

- Source of fighting
- Have led to a breakup
- We've all become friends
- I haven't given myself fully to my new lover
- An ex has actively interfered in my new life
- Feedback from my ex has helped me understand myself in a new relationship
- Continuing a friendship with my ex has hurt my new lover
- The friendship with my ex has been supportive of my new relationship
- Other . . .

3. If you had the chance, would you make a different choice about remaining friends with any of your exes than you made in the past? Yes? No? Ask yourself: For what reason would I make a different choice? What choice would I make?

4. Be willing to handle the friendship with your ex without damaging your new relationship.

- Your main allegiance needs to be with your present lover, not your ex-lover
- You need to be clear with your new lover about why you broke up with your ex and why you want to remain friends
- The three of you need to be able to spend some time together so that your lover and your ex have a real impression of each other
- There can be no secrecy about contact with your ex

- If your ex looks at you, talks to you, or
  writes to you like a lover, the limits of
  your friendship need to be clearly
  established

You Don't Want to Remain Friends with Your Ex

If you don't want to maintain a friendship with your
ex, here are some suggestions that will help you be
clear about your position with yourself, with her, and
with the people in your lives.

Painful breakups. In many breakups, one person
wants to end it and the other wants to work to
improve the relationship. The pain of rejection may
be too great to allow the possibility of friendship.
Both people should be allowed to have their feelings.

Dishonest breakups. Honesty is the basis of
friendship. If one or both people have failed to
acknowledge the reasons for the ending, there is no
foundation for true friendship.

Complications of a new relationship. When
feelings of jealousy or competition are strong between
an ex and current lover, some people choose to
simplify their lives by eliminating contact with the
ex.

New perceptions of the ex. It may happen that
during the lover relationship or during the breakup,
one or both people lose interest or respect for the
other, and a friendship is no longer possible.

Communication is just as important at this junc-
ture in your relationship as any preceding time. You
can eliminate anxiety and confusion by being clear

with each other about what to expect in terms of friendship. This means stating clearly whether you intend to see her; to call her, to acknowledge her birthday, other special times, or crises in her life.

Phase Three: New Life

In phase three you have each settled into a new life, whether as a single or with a new partner. Both people will experience internal peace in this phase if they have grieved and accepted the breakup on an emotional level and if they understand why the breakup occurred.

The challenges of this phase are

- To take responsibility for one's own feelings
- To accept the ex-lover's new life

Mikela and Latasha ended a seven-year relationship eight months ago. Mikela had wanted to go to couples therapy rather than end, but Latasha refused. They had spent six months in therapy two years ago and had rapidly experienced the same problems again.

Mikela was bitter and widely exposed Latasha's unwillingness to get help in their community. Now she says, "I really saw myself as a victim back then. Now I'm sad because Latasha is a great woman and I miss her. She's living with someone else, and I'm not. But we were never a good match, and I kept trying to make her be what I needed. I still cry, but I also hope that she's happy. And I have an interesting blind date on Saturday."

The more honesty that existed in the relationship and during the breakup, the more likely it is that the couple will handle the challenges of phase three.

The way you deal with ex-lovers will have an impact on your life. Knowing the significant stages that take place as you change from lovers to ex-lovers will enable you to handle the decisions that have to be made and the important issues that have to be faced during this transition time.

Chapter 9:

The Healing Quality of Relationships

What is a healing relationship? It is one in which something that was missing from childhood is now experienced, or something that was painful in childhood is now soothed. A healing relationship therefore can be very intense, as one partner (it may be both) finds comfort for childhood wounds.

The experiences we have growing up inevitably have an impact upon us and affect our adult lives. Everyone has experienced some moments of insensitivity or neglect. However, if you generally had childhood experiences that made you feel good about yourself and also made you feel emotionally safe, then

you have a good chance of forming deep and rewarding relationships as an adult.

A person who didn't have a supportive foundation
is likely to have more relationship trouble and may
not realize that it is her early experiences that compromise her adult relationships.

Childhood experiences can influence the kind of
partner you choose, whether you choose a partner at
all, and how you function in a relationship.

One of the benefits of a loving adult relationship
is that some healing of childhood pain can take place.
But isn't a woman who plays a role in healing her
partner codependent, keenly needing the other woman
to need her? If the primary or sole bond in the
relationship is serving the early unmet needs of the
partner, the answer is yes. But healing that is woven
into the fabric of a rich and more complete relationship can be a positive aspect of the relationship.
Many couples interact in ways that contribute to
healing childhood wounds.

Children are set up to have difficult adult relationships by (a) experiences they should have had,
but didn't, or (b) by experiences they shouldn't have
had, and did.

Following are some of the things that can create
emotional wounds that are carried into adulthood.

Deficits in childhood
　　Lack of love
　　Lack of emotional support
　　Lack of physical or spoken affection
　　Lack of guidance
　　Lack of limits
　　Lack of involvement

Lack of material items

Childhood wounds
  Loss of significant people
  Loss of home
  Shame
  Harsh criticism
  Humiliation
  Physical abuse
  Sexual abuse

If you are aware of the impact your childhood has had on you, and if you have a plan for dealing with the effect on your emotions and behavior, the problems that inevitably occur in any relationship will be easier to handle. If however, your childhood pain is exposed for the first time within a relationship, emotional turbulence is inevitable.

Susie and Vanessa had been in a committed relationship for a year, but the early optimism about building a life together was quickly disappearing. Their fights ended in frustration, and they felt distant more and more of the time. They loved each other, so why was this happening?

As Susie and Vanessa reacted to each other, they were blind to the fact that the conflict between them had to do with pain that started long ago in their family experiences.

Susie's parents were emotionally cold, and very little affection was ever shown in the family. When Vanessa showed warmth by touching Susie frequently during the day, Susie didn't see this as an uncomplicated expression of affection. She felt that Vanessa was being demanding.

Vanessa's upbringing had included frequent harsh criticism from her mother. No matter how hard she tried, the young Vanessa could never seem to be the child her mother wanted. As an adult, Vanessa was hypersensitive to any comments Susie might make about her, so she overreacted.

Susie is an example of someone entering a relationship who has a childhood deficit — in her case, lack of love. Displays of affection feel foreign and excessive to her, and she doesn't know how to react appropriately.

Vanessa is an example of someone bringing childhood wounds into a relationship. The excessive criticism she received makes it hard for her to hear any comments about any aspect of herself. Attempts at joint problem-solving are painful and ineffective. She reacts to anything negative as if it is a personal rebuke.

Recognizing that there was something more to their conflict than the day-to-day disagreements any couple has, Vanessa and Susie sought professional guidance. Each realized that she was asking the other woman to be a loving partner *and* to be the affectionate, supportive parent she had never had.

Susie and Vanessa were able to contribute to each other's healing because of significant shared emotional experiences. Some things need to be experienced for healing to take place. Susie read about warmth and the safe, trusting feeling that develops in a loving relationship. She kept a journal and put into words her grief about not having affection in her early years and her discomfort with physical closeness now.

Sharing her feelings about this with a counselor was an essential step. But only when she experienced herself letting go in Vanessa's arms and being able to feel safe and warm and loved did she feel changed.

Vanessa took a personal development class, learning how she had internalized the harsh criticism of her mother. She realized that she had come to view herself the way her mother had seen her as a child. Vanessa began to understand how she had projected her mother's attitudes onto her lover, so that she saw Susie's comments as criticisms. Vanessa learned techniques to help her not to overreact and worked with a therapist to release her hidden anger at her mother. At home she experienced Susie's patience and acceptance while she learned to listen to Susie commenting on her behavior. She found she could listen and hear only Susie's voice. Vanessa had come to trust that Susie loved and respected her as a person, and she was healed inside.

These freeing emotional experiences have created an intense emotional bond. Both Vanessa and Susie now feel the delightful feelings lovers experience when they are accepted and loved. And for the first time they both feel an emotional openness that is safe and flowing. Their efforts have provided a mutually healing experience.

If both people in a couple come from supportive, nurturing families, they will bring few wounds and deficits into their adult relationships. It will be quite normal for them to expect from each other such things as love, support, involvement, protection, and sharing of material items.

However, if either (or both) enters a relationship

wounded or with a serious lack from childhood, the need and longing for what is missing will be intense. Such couples knowingly or unknowingly make contracts with each other to make up for what they lacked as children.

There are several types of contracts (agreements) that these couples design. The danger is that the contract may not be spoken. And because it is never actually put into words, there is no conscious and open agreement between the two people. An unspoken contract is like a minefield ready to explode without warning. If one woman in a relationship believes there is an important unspoken agreement that has been broken, the results can be disastrous.

If a woman is *unaware* of what she wants from her partner, desires of which she is unconscious will become the basis of an unspoken contract. If a woman is *aware* of what she wants from her partner but neglects to say it or is unwilling to say it, her withheld desires also become the basis of an unspoken contract.

Women who are aware of what they need and are willing to state their needs form spoken contracts, the advantage being that both partners clearly understand the agreement.

It seems obvious that it is better to make sure that each person states explicitly what she expects and needs from the relationship. However, many times the wounds and deficits from childhood create the terms of an unspoken contract. And because the wants and needs are out of the awareness of one or both people, the fact that this unspoken agreement even exists comes to light through disappointments and frustration.

Relationship Contracts

There are four main types of relationship contracts that result from childhood pain: successful unspoken contract, unsuccessful unspoken contract, successful spoken contract, and unsuccessful spoken contract.

Successful Unspoken Contract

"I am healing you while you are healing me."

It sometimes happens that without conscious awareness or discussion of what each person needs, each one will attempt to give the other what she needs. What each woman needs links wordlessly with what the other has to offer.

"I want to feel this forever" is expressed at some point. After a time, however, healing takes place, and the needs of a wounded, deprived child are replaced by a wider range of adult needs. The lovers may not understand what is happening, but they feel the difference. At this stage a crisis occurs in the relationship.

Teresa and Winona met at a friend's home, and both experienced an immediate, intense connection. They began seeing each other the next day and within a week Winona was spending every night at Teresa's apartment. They each believed that they had discovered an extraordinary love. Winona felt more open and trusting than she had at any other time in her life.

Teresa had had a lifelong dream of a career in

interior design, but she had felt emotionally unable to pursue the necessary studies. She also did not have enough money to live and go to school at the same time. Within months of meeting Winona, Teresa began an educational program that would fulfill her dreams.

The healing portion of their relationship lasted six years. It was a time of emotional intensity previously unknown to either woman. Winona gave both financial support and emotional nourishment to Teresa, called her frequently through the day, and had long evening conversations about how to manage her problems and schoolwork.

For Winona's part, she had become so expert at guarding her heart that she was not even aware of how she kept herself closed until she met Teresa. The safety she felt in the presence of Teresa's gentle, sensitive manner amazed her. Winona found herself able to receive affection and tenderness and learned to be playful.

They were both sure that they had found their life partner and that nothing could interrupt their happiness. What neither took into account was the influence their childhoods had had upon them. Both Teresa and Winona had grown up in emotionally depriving families. Teresa had never received emotional support and encouragement, and her talents and abilities had never been recognized. Winona had been beaten as a child and continually criticized. She could not remember ever being touched tenderly.

Their relationship was intense and joyous at the beginning because Winona and Teresa did for each other what their families had not done for them.

The week after their sixth anniversary, Winona

became the director of the international division of her engineering firm. This new position meant that Winona had to travel extensively during the next three years, and Teresa took a leave of absence from her design program, supposedly so that she could manage their home and finances in Winona's frequent absences.

At year seven of the relationship, Winona was diagnosed with diabetes. Her doctor assured her that with proper diet and exercise she could manage her illness without medication. For the next two years, however, Winona failed to adopt the necessary health practices. Her health deteriorated, and she needed to use insulin injections.

Neither Winona nor Teresa realized that they had been healing each other as well as loving each other for six years and that external circumstances had pushed them out of the healing phase. Neither anticipated the crisis that would follow.

Teresa noticed she was tired every day and would cry for no apparent reason. Winona began to feel irritated with Teresa's moods, although she struggled against her feelings.

Teresa was becoming depressed because she had not yet learned to support herself emotionally in the way Winona did. Winona's absences made her feel like an abandoned child. Teresa also felt she had somehow failed Winona, because Winona's health had worsened.

On Christmas eve of the ninth year of their relationship, Winona watched Teresa talking with a woman who had recently moved to town. Over the next weeks, Teresa saw Zoe and insisted that they were just friends and that she was merely helping "the new woman in town."

On Valentine's Day both women felt strained and distant. Winona confronted the change in their relationship, and Teresa acknowledged that she was thinking about leaving.

Their relationship was in crisis, but *not* because of depression or diabetes or Zoe. Each woman had been basking in the good feelings created by her partner's nurturing. Neither had moved past the point of receiving what they had missed. They were like children with good parents, who are reluctant to grow up and assume the responsibility of self-care. Neither Teresa nor Winona were doing for themselves what they were doing for each other, and each was feeling burdened.

They did not break up at this point. Several of their friends encouraged them to seek counseling to at least unravel the mystery of their difficulties. In a year and a half of counseling, they began to see how they had been healing each other's childhood pain. A new relationship was forged as they learned to manage their own emotional and physical needs.

Teresa came to accept that she was important to Winona without taking care of her. Winona struggled to learn that Teresa could manage her own problems and still love her.

Teresa elected to work as a receptionist in a design firm and finish school one class at a time. Winona joined a support group for people with chronic illness to learn how to manage her diabetes effectively.

Both women remember the exquisite pleasure of discovery in their early years together. Both acknowledge that they sometimes wish they could feel that way again, although they realize that the intensity of feeling came in large part from the healing process they were experiencing. Now they have begun to experience the deep satisfactions of two independent, loving women sharing their lives.

Unsuccessful Unspoken Contract

"I thought you would heal me, and I'm angry that you haven't."

Once again, there is no conscious awareness of the agreement the partners have made, but the contract exists in their inner worlds, just as if it had been drawn up by an attorney. Expectations result.

Debbie and Odell are an example of a couple who have entered into an unsuccessful unspoken contract. Debbie, like Teresa, needs to accept more support from others. Her parents disguised their coldness by proclaiming that they were raising each of their four children to be self-sufficient. In reality, the children were deprived of warmth, and Debbie learned to be guarded and expect rejection.

Odell is an example of the results of over-indulging a child. Her family did not expect her to manage her own life. Now, as an adult, she neglects her finances and fails to pursue activities she knows will make her feel good about herself.

When Debbie and Odell first met there was an instant attraction, partly on a sexual level. Unconsciously, Debbie and Odell recognized in the other the qualities that could help each one heal.

Odell was warm and willing to be helpful, but Debbie was unable to let Odell get close. Debbie sought therapy but could not navigate the waters of her own mistrust.

Debbie loved Odell but would not indulge her by doing for her what Odell needed to do for herself. Instead of appreciating Debbie's love and respect for Odell's abilities, Odell made demands and threw tantrums in the expectation that Debbie would relent.

Always fearing rejection, Debbie felt increasingly isolated behind the wall she had built between her own needs and Odell. In turn, Odell felt continually frustrated because she was clinging to her refusal to assume responsibility for herself.

This couple ultimately broke up because neither was fulfilling the unspoken contract they had between them.

Successful Spoken Contract

"Based on our early experiences, we each know what we need and are willing to give it to each other."

Hannah and Meryl have had a relationship for three years. The first four months were stormy and frightening. They talked a lot about their frustrations, sought professional counseling, kept journals about their feelings, and problem-solved together. They both feel they have created a successful relationship based on a spoken contract to heal each other.

Each one has her own apartment. Hannah is aware of how she felt intruded upon by her alcoholic mother, who destroyed her privacy by demanding to know what Hannah was thinking, checking on her mail and telephone calls, and even going through her personal things. As an adult, Hannah is clear that having an independent space and sleeping alone some nights each week gives her a sense of separateness that frees her emotionally.

Although Meryl would prefer more contact, Hannah has explained her strong feelings about maintaining a separate space, and Meryl is able to accept this, thus giving Hannah something she hasn't had before — a sense of respect for her need for privacy and time alone.

On Meryl's side, she was under-appreciated in her family. When she began the relationship with Hannah, she felt painful doubts as to why Hannah would love her. "Hannah's so attractive and smart. Why would she want me?"

Hannah is secure in the love she and Meryl share, without much verbal reassurance. However she is sensitive to what Meryl missed in her childhood and now longs for — appreciation of herself as a valuable, deserving person. She frequently tells Meryl how much she cares for her, acknowledges Meryl's business skills, and comments on her beautiful eyes and hands. For the first time Meryl feels bathed in the warmth of love and appreciation.

As their relationship progresses over three years, Hannah is finding that she needs less time alone. She feels more trust, realizing that she can request privacy without requiring geographical distance.

Hannah talks with Meryl about the possibility of living together within the next six months.

Meryl loves the reassurance Hannah gives her, but she is finding she is no longer so frantic about receiving it every day.

In addition to the work they do to heal each other, Meryl and Hannah find other ways to connect. They take sailing lessons, have a large group of friends, and enjoy cooking together on weekends.

Unsuccessful Spoken Contract

"Based on our early experiences, we each know what we need, but we are unable to give it to each other."

Gemma and Coral ended their three-year relationship frustrated and disappointed. In the first months they were together they locked horns regularly and hurt each other's feelings, though neither intended to damage the other person. The intensity of their fighting was confusing to them.

Both women sought counseling to understand what they were bringing from childhood into their relationship. They talked openly about what they had learned about themselves, finding that each was very much like the other woman's mother.

Gemma's mother had been self-involved and demeaning. Coral's mother had frightened Coral by constant yelling and temper tantrums.

Jointly deciding that this was an opportunity to heal and learn new ways of responding, they tried to change their behaviors and react differently to each other. Over months they sought the support of friends and attended a workshop for couples.

Both felt they were reexperiencing the same pain that had made their childhoods unbearable. Had they had little external stress during their three years together, it is possible they might have been successful in helping each other heal. But Coral lost her job, Gemma's sister died, and both women had illnesses.

They had clearly communicated their needs:

Gemma: I need you to make positive statements to me, to encourage me, and to believe in me.
Coral: I need you to express your feelings to me without raising your voice or getting out of control.

Despite genuine effort and use of external support, Gemma and Coral were unable to change their way of interacting and chose to end their relationship.

The effect of a healing experience on a total relationship depends on two factors: (a) Do both people have lives outside the relationship? This may include family, friends, work, hobbies, and children. (b) Does the couple share with each other in ways other than the healing experience? This might mean creating a home or sharing children, hobbies, pets, social life, community work.

If the relationship exists exclusively or primarily for healing, it will be emotionally intense, possessive, and nurturing, and it will eventually end.

If healing is part of a fuller relationship, it will transform as the two women need each other less to experience healing. These couples struggle, learn, and grow together, ending up feeling they have contributed to making each other whole.

For some couples the only reason to be together is to heal childhood pain. They may not be suited to be long-term partners because they are too different in terms of goals, background, lifestyle, age, interests, or values.

Such relationships should not be viewed as inappropriate or as failures. Both people have had an experience that may make it possible to have a complete relationship in the future. The intense sense of loss during the crisis can be mitigated if both people can come to understand the very necessary contract they made and completed together.

For other couples, the healing experience is but one phase in their relationship. When the healing is somewhat completed, the relationship goes into crisis and transforms. They move to the position of two separate and involved people who are now strong enough to maintain their relationship with each other and with the outer world.

Shared
and
Independent
Activities

Healing Childhood Pain

Some relationships exist primarily for healing

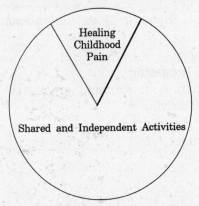

Any full and satisfying relationship contains some elements of healing.

Healing in a Relationship

If your relationship is intensely emotional, or if you feel you are being nurtured in a way you never have before, you may be in a relationship that exists, at least partly, for healing.

What brings about healing in a relationship?
Acceptance
- Warmth and comfort
- Experiencing together what was not experienced in childhood, such as sharing feelings, playfulness, positive feedback, support, encouragement, holding, and reassurance

What, apart from a love relationship, promotes healing?
- Therapy
- 12-step programs
- Participation in spiritual programs
- Journal writing
- Supportive relationships
- Mentoring
- Education

How would I know if I am likely to seek healing in a relationship?
- I am easily wounded
- I neglect self-care
- I need frequent reassurance about my partner's love for me
- I am frequently angry at my partner, or disappointed in her, although she doesn't do anything seriously wrong

What can I do to help myself and my relationship grow and continue beyond the time of healing?
- Learn to do for yourself what your partner does for you. This may include believing in yourself, encouraging yourself, helping yourself remember your strengths and successes, doing nurturing things for yourself.
- Take in the positive comments your partner makes about you. Hold them in your mind and heart. Refer to them.
- Learn to do the tasks your lover does for you. Even if she continues to do them, be able to do them yourself.

- Make sure you each have at least one
  other important relationship in addition to
  the one the two of you share.
- Be able to adequately support yourself eco-
  nomically.
- Learn to tolerate each other's need for
  separate time and activities.
- Be able to distinguish between appreciating
  and enjoying your lover's meeting your
  needs, and *expecting* her to do this.
- Have a plan of good self-care and follow it.
  This should include diet, rest, exercise,
  recreation, relaxation, and management of
  time, money, resources, and health.
- Acknowledge to yourself, and if you choose
  to, to your lover, whatever unmet needs
  and pain you bring into your relationship
  from childhood.
- Seek professional counseling for guidance or
  management of unresolved childhood issues.

Everyone brings something painful from their
childhood into adult life and relationships. These
childhood pains compromise full participation in life.
Some healing of childhood pain can take place in an
adult relationship. The relationship is likely to endure
if the couple connects in significant ways in addition
to the need for healing.

Chapter 10:

Lessons Learned from Past Relationships

Experience is a great teacher. Reflection on the joy and pain you experienced in each of your significant past relationships offers insight into who you are in your personal interactions and how you can behave more lovingly toward yourself and a future partner.

Past Relationships

If you think of past relationships as failures, it may help you to:

Acknowledge that all people have different

needs at different stages in their lives. It's possible a past lover really was right for an individual at that particular time. Specific needs were met in a positive way, but when these were no longer needed, perhaps it was best for both people to move on.

Look at life as a series of learning experiences. One way to look at life is that it is a series of learning experiences. Review what happened in the relationship. Women in our culture are socialized to be victims, so it is very easy to slip into a victim posture at the end of a relationship: "Look how she hurt me/deceived me." Acknowledgment that both partners contributed to the situation is vital to accepting personal responsibility, and thus beginning the learning process.

If you believe that from the beginning of adulthood you are fully formed and set in the way you will live your life, each relationship difficulty or ending will be analyzed with the question, "What is wrong with me?"

If you look at life experiences as opportunities to learn and grow, however, relationship struggles become a source of information about yourself and about new paths to explore.

Some lesbians choose to continue learning with one partner, changing their relationship over a long span of time. Others choose to leave and use what they have learned in time spent alone, or in a new relationship.

When a lesbian couple who have been seeing each other for less than a year break up, they each feel they have lost a relationship. In fact, they are still in a getting-to-know-you period. Relationships have definite stages: (a) during the first three months each person tends to be careful to show the best of herself; (b) three months to a year covers a period of learning to deal with realities — what the other person is really like; (c) it is only after a year that consolidation of the relationship can begin to take place.

Realize that building a real relationship takes time. Lesbians may view their relationships as unstable because they shift to a new person after a year or less. Rethinking the experience would include the insight that you need to spend a significant amount of time getting to know someone before committing to a relationship. Brief relationships are therefore a necessary, though frustrating, part of finding an appropriate partner.

Gain information from past lovers. Past lovers are a valuable source of information, both about what makes us desirable as partners and also about what qualities make relationships with us difficult.

Not all feedback is necessarily accurate. A past lover's perception could be distorted for many reasons, including anger, resentment, and jealousy.

If you are not clear that a perception a past lover has told you is accurate, ask some other people who have known you for more than five years. Should more than two past lovers have shared exactly the same perception of you, it is likely there is truth in it.

As an exercise, list in chronological order the name of any woman with whom you've had a relationship lasting more than three months. As best you can, remember and write down the feedback each woman gave you about what was difficult for her in relating to you, or anything she thinks you could have done to make the relationship better.

Learn from parents' relationship. If, as a child, you've had a good example of any particular adult behavior, you're going to have an easier time learning that behavior yourself.

This is true in relationships as well as in other aspects of life. There are limits to how much can be learned from parents' example, however. Parents can teach and model the importance of values that support good relationships — honesty, commitment, patience, perseverance. They can demonstrate such positive things as communicative and affectionate behavior, problem-solving, and the sharing of time and responsibilities.

But parents are of their generation, not yours, and they are affected by the social standards, attitudes, political and historic events that occurred during their lives. They can only offer you what their experience has given to them, and it must be different from yours. You need to use your judgment and your observations of your contemporaries' relationships to guide you in applying what you learned from your parents' relationship.

How Do I Learn from Past Relationships?

When you become aware of what you can gain from past relationships, self-knowledge increases and you have the opportunity to initiate constructive changes.

Awareness. Most people have a clear awareness of the pain that occurs at the ending of a relationship. But a more constructive awareness that leads to greater insight is the attitude "I'm going to figure out my part, and her part, in getting me to this painful place and then do my best to change my part in the future."

Statements like "She was just a bitch" or "I was such a jerk" or "We just grew apart" need to be replaced with the more thoughtful "She didn't start out a bitch" and "I didn't start out a jerk" and "We were once close."

Ask, "How did we each contribute to the change?" The answer to this question will come from a willingness to observe, to remember, to seek and accept feedback, and to think about cause and effect.

The following questions will help with awareness.

- What is one time I remember the relationship changing for the worse?
- What had been happening between us just prior to the change? Were we communicating well? Were we dealing with the ways in which we are different? Were we learning something new about each other? Were we facing something that has been difficult in the past? Were either of us experiencing high levels of stress?
- What was happening with me at the time of the change? Was I fatigued, ill, premenstrual? Was I experiencing anything particularly difficult with my friends, family, job?
- What was happening with her at the time

of the change? Was she fatigued, ill, premenstrual? Was she experiencing anything
difficult with her friends, family, job?

Some examples of awareness that you might gain
are "I am impatient whenever my lover is ill"; "We
fight the day before her parents are coming to visit";
"I am cold to her when she goes out with friends
and doesn't include me"; "I attack when I feel criticized"; "When she is angry, I think it's my fault."
Analysis of your interaction includes two parts:
what happens, and your reaction to what happens.

**Expanding information you have about your-
self.** Once you have an awareness, you can expand
your information about yourself. Begin with an
interest and curiosity about your reactions to tense
situations in past and present relationships. Examples
are: "I am impatient whenever my lover is ill." Did
my family get irritated with me when I was ill as a
child? Did I have an ill parent, and could I be
bringing my anger about that parent to my lover? Do
I let myself have attention when I am ill?

Insight: My irritation is telling me something
about myself.

Constructive change: When my lover is ill, I must
remember that I bring my own unrelated feelings to
the situation. I will learn to calm myself and talk to
her about what would make her feel cared about
when she is ill.

"We fight the day before her parents come to
visit."

Her parents were here Thanksgiving, Easter, and
last Wednesday — and we had a fight each time. If
she gets tense before they come, am I supportive and

calm, or do I also get tense? Am I jealous of the attention her parents give her? Can I be myself around them? Do I feel they accept me and our relationship? Do I have feelings about my own parents that I could be bringing into the situation?

Insight: My part in the fighting is telling me something about myself.

Constructive change: I will learn to manage my tension when my lover's parents come to visit. I can learn not to react to her tension. We can have a conversation about the situation before her parents visit.

"I am cold to her when she goes out with friends and doesn't include me." She went bowling Thursday night with work friends, and I wouldn't snuggle when she came home. I don't even like bowling. Is it hard for me to accept that she gets some of her needs met apart from me? Were either of my parents cold to me when I left home or had my own interests and life? Am I insecure about being lovable? Do I have trouble saying if I'm jealous? If I sincerely wanted to spend time with my lover, could I tell her? If I'm angry, do I act cold rather than saying how I feel?

Insight: My coldness is telling me something about myself.

Constructive change: I can learn to trust that I am important to my lover. I can learn to express my irritation with words, rather than angry behavior.

"I attack when I feel criticized." My lover sometimes tells me she doesn't like the way I talk to her or do my part around the house. She could be gentler in her style, but no matter how she tells me, I attack. Do I expect myself to be perfect? Am I self-critical? Do I feel ashamed of myself for having any flaws? Was I criticized harshly as a child?

Insight: My strong reaction to criticism tells me something about myself.

Constructive change: I can become more comfortable with my faults and flaws. The more I accept myself, the less I will react to criticism.

"When she is angry, I think it's always my fault." My lover has assured me that if she's angry at me she'll tell me. Nonetheless, if I hear her swear in the other room or see an angry look on her face, I ask her what I've done and worry about her leaving me. Do I take responsibility for many things that are not mine, like other people's work problems? Do I seek peace at all costs? Do I feel undeserving of what I want or need in life? Were either of my parents practicing alcoholics? Were my parents blamers or abusive to me in some way?

Insight: My taking responsibility for my lover's anger tells me something about myself.

Constructive change: I will learn to relax when my lover is angry. I will learn more about how my parents' behavior affected my sense of security and self-esteem.

By observing the interaction between you and your lover, and by taking responsibility for your part in the interaction, it is possible to develop a plan for constructive change.

What Can Past Relationships Teach Me?

When a relationship ends, the pain of the loss can be a strong motivation to review the relationship and use the lessons learned to prevent similar pain in the future.

Using the following fourteen points, check your responses to each of the following areas:

I have learned from my past relationships that I need to grow in the areas of . . .

☐ Partner selection
☐ Realistic expectations of a relationship
☐ Managing conflict
☐ Communicating what I need
☐ Managing my life
☐ Sexual behavior
☐ Paying attention to my partner
☐ Affection
☐ Communicating my anger
☐ Doing my share
☐ Dealing with friends
☐ Dealing with family
☐ Dealing with money
☐ Dealing with my physical and emotional health

My experience in my past relationships has helped me grow in the following areas . . .

☐ Partner selection
☐ Realistic expectations of a relationship
☐ Managing conflict
☐ Communicating what I need
☐ Managing my life
☐ Sexual behavior
☐ Paying attention to my partner
☐ Affection

☐ Communicating my anger
☐ Doing my share
☐ Dealing with friends
☐ Dealing with family
☐ Dealing with money
☐ Dealing with my physical and emotional health

My experience in my past relationships indicates that the most vital area(s) for me to grow and change are . . .

☐ Partner selection
☐ Realistic expectations of a relationship
☐ Managing conflict
☐ Communicating what I need
☐ Managing my life
☐ Sexual behavior
☐ Paying attention to my partner
☐ Affection
☐ Communicating my anger
☐ Doing my share
☐ Dealing with friends
☐ Dealing with family
☐ Dealing with money
☐ Dealing with my physical and emotional health

Finishing Relationships

When two people stop seeing each other, they may both have unresolved feelings about themselves, each other, and the relationship. Willing something to be over does not make unfinished feelings go away. Unfinished feelings can affect your sense of well-being, your health, and your ability to connect deeply with a new lover.

Two steps complete the emotional work of a breakup, (a) evaluation and (b) finishing feelings.

Use the following checklist to learn a helpful process to carry out these two steps. Answer for your most recent breakup, and then complete the checklist for all significant relationships you have had in the past.

1. Evaluating Your Relationship

Relationship with ....
Month(s) year(s) of the relationship ....
I was ......(age at the beginning of the relationship)

When I first met her, I was attracted to

I started a relationship with her because

During the relationship the best things were

When I remember the good things I feel

During the relationship the most difficult things were

When I remember the difficult things I feel

I / She / We both broke up the relationship

At the time of the breakup I thought the reason for ending was

Now I believe the reason we ended was

In the FIRST MONTH after the breakup (answer *yes* or *no*)

	YES	NO
I was in shock	☐	☐
I felt sad	☐	☐
I cried	☐	☐
I felt scared	☐	☐
I talked about my fears	☐	☐
I talked about my anger	☐	☐
I reminisced about the relationship	☐	☐
I reached out to friends or family for support	☐	☐
I avoided dating	☐	☐
I spent some time alone	☐	☐

In the FIRST THREE MONTHS after the breakup (answer *yes* or *no*)

	YES	NO
I sometimes felt sad	☐	☐
I sometimes cried	☐	☐
I sometimes felt angry	☐	☐
I talked about my anger	☐	☐
I reminisced about the relationship	☐	☐
I reached out to family or friends for companion-ship	☐	☐

	YES	NO
I sometimes had fun	☐	☐
I felt relieved	☐	☐

From FOURTH MONTH after the breakup to the ONE YEAR anniversary of the breakup (answer *yes* or *no*)

	YES	NO
I sometimes felt sad	☐	☐
I occasionally cried	☐	☐
I sometimes felt angry	☐	☐
I expressed my anger	☐	☐
I gained a sense of my part in the relationship's failure	☐	☐
I increasingly enjoyed my life	☐	☐
I began to believe I could trust someone again	☐	☐
I could acknowledge what was good in the relationship	☐	☐
At some point since the breakup I have talked with or written to my ex about our relationship and my feelings about the breakup	☐	☐
I reached a time when I could comfortably be in the same place as my ex-lover	☐	☐
I gained at least one specific learning from the relationship that will help me in the future	☐	☐

If my relationship lasted MORE THAN TWO YEARS, from time to time, after the first year of grief (answer *yes* or *no*)

	YES	NO
I dreamed about my ex	☐	☐
I missed my ex	☐	☐
I felt angry	☐	☐
I felt sad	☐	☐

I remembered the good times   □   □
I occasionally talked about her   □   □
I came to see both the positive and negative
  impact the relationship had on my life   □   □

KEY Each *yes* answer indicates a normal feeling
or experience that leads to a genuine finishing of a
relationship. Each *no* answer suggests some unfinished business you have from the relationship.

If you answered *no* **1– 4** times, you're doing a
good job of finishing relationships. Your *no* answers
will indicate what steps to take to enhance your
already adequate style of dealing with the ending of a
relationship.

If you answered *no* **5–10** times, your style of
ending a relationship is incomplete. You may have
experienced moods (sad or irritable), physical difficulties (fatigue, headaches, muscle pain, loss of
libido), and troubles with attachment (either too
quickly or too guardedly) as a result.

If you answered *no* **11–20** times, you have unfinished business that has very likely affected you
negatively, as well as harmed any relationship that
followed.

If you answered *no* **21 or more** times, you have
already experienced a health or relationship crisis or
you will at some time in your life. Therapy or counseling will help you understand how you are harming
yourself and sabotaging your relationships.

2. How to Finish a Past Relationship

Finishing past relationships is a combination of
awareness, expression, learning, and time.

Awareness. The following questions will help you increase your awareness about how and why your breakups occur.

Think about each significant breakup in your life. List the reasons for each breakup. Does the same reason recur? If the same reason occurs more than twice, you are not learning the lesson relationships are presenting to you.

How many times did *you* end a relationship?

How many times did your *partner* end it?

If your relationships frequently end and you would like a relationship to endure, you need to take more time to get to know a potential partner. If your partner usually initiates the breakup, you need to learn more about your part in creating an unsatisfactory relationship. Ask your ex-lover for a frank discussion.

I see the following things about myself that have made relationships difficult

More than one partner has told me that the following things about me are difficult in a relationship

My most recent partner told me that the following things about me were difficult in our relationship

   Expression. The following questions will help you identify how adequately you expressed your feelings and needs during your breakups. Expression of feelings promotes healing, and expression of needs increases the probability that you will have adequate support while the healing takes place.

During the relationship I had trouble talking to my lover about

When I broke up with her I felt sad about

. . . scared about

. . . angry about

When I broke up with her I cried / talked about my anger / talked about my fears

I didn't reach out to people because

When I broke up with her, I missed

I never communicated directly with her about my feelings
because

The things I want to do differently in my next
relationship are (check each statement that applies):

☐ Get to know her better before committing
☐ Take more risks with honest communication
☐ Make time for the relationship
☐ Take better care of myself
☐ Open my heart more fully
☐ Take care of the other relationships in my life
☐ Take responsibility for solving my individual problems
☐ Maintain a sexual relationship
☐ Seek guidance when I can't work out a problem
☐ Other

When you have finished the above section on
Expression, consider whether you would be willing to
contact your ex-lover and share your thoughts and
feelings directly. If not, consider sharing what you
have written with someone — friend, relative,
therapist, spiritual advisor.

Time. After a breakup, I need to give myself time
alone and time with supportive people before I date
or get involved with someone new. I have avoided
this necessary healing time in the past because (check
each statement that applies)

☐ I was lonely
☐ I was afraid of being alone
☐ I wanted to avoid grieving
☐ My ego was wounded

☐ I met a good person and thought I would lose her if I
   waited
☐ I wanted comfort
☐ I wanted to "show" my ex
☐ I missed sex
☐ I didn't know I needed time to heal

Be willing to give yourself the necessary healing
time, should you experience another breakup. Finishing a relationship emotionally is relieving, and it
creates space for new loving feelings.

Guidelines for Getting It
Right Next Time

1. Don't date anyone who has been out of a
relationship fewer than three months.
2. Don't commit to anyone who has been out of a
relationship less than a year.
3. Don't commit to a person who has experienced
the death of someone significant in her life until
after the first year of grieving.
4. Honestly review your last lover's complaints
about you. Even if she is angry and exaggerates,
there is probably some truth in her complaints. Plan
to correct what she validly complained about and be
prepared to share your flaws — and your efforts to
change — with your next partner.
5. If you have had several failed relationships
with the same type of person, stand back and
evaluate yourself objectively. Why are you repeating
the same mistake? Look at each relationship for
similarities. Is something being repeated in each rela-

tionship? Is there a similarity of personality, or of the way she made you feel, or of the way she treated other people? Do you find yourself always being drawn to someone with the same flaws? Are your reactions in each relationship the same?

Repeating a pattern is often a clue that you are trying to resolve a painful relationship that occurred with someone from your childhood. A conversation with a counselor or therapist may help clear up the mystery.

Chapter 11:

Relationships in Danger

Is your relationship in danger? Answer *yes* or *no* to the following questions:

	YES	NO
1. Are you unhappy more than half of the time?	☐	☐
2. Are you considering having an affair?	☐	☐
3. Are you defensive with your lover?	☐	☐
4. Do you feel resentful about things you haven't told your lover?	☐	☐
5. Do you feel emotionally distant from your lover?	☐	☐

6. Have you lost interest in sex with each
   other?   ☐   ☐
7. Are you less interested in spending time
   together?   ☐   ☐
8. Do you often feel critical of your lover?   ☐   ☐
9. Is one (or both of you) frequently angry?   ☐   ☐
10. Do you frequently think about ending the
    relationship?   ☐   ☐

KEY Total your *yes* answers.

1–2 It's time to have an open discussion about the relationship and how to make it better.

3– 4 Be honest with yourself about your commitment to revitalize the relationship. Is there enough in the relationship that you value? State to each other the specific changes you feel you need from each other. Seek support from friends and guidance from a spiritual leader or a counselor.

5– 6 Have a frank discussion with each other about whether it is worthwhile to each of you to continue. There is hard work ahead, and you both need to be willing to do it. Seek professional help.

7–10 The relationship is in crisis, and this situation may be irreversible. Review for yourself whether or not you have had your needs met to a satisfactory degree for at least half the life of the relationship. Think back. Did you have serious concerns about the relationship from the beginning? The lack of reward in the relationship is a serious issue that must be addressed immediately or the relationship will not survive.

Pay particular attention to questions 1 and 10. People who are unhappy more than half of the time, or who frequently think about breaking up, are likely to end their relationships.

Yes answers occur when a relationship is in danger. It is important to know that a depressive illness could lead to the same answers. If either you or your partner answered *yes* more than two times, you could be experiencing a clinical depression. Reading Colleen Dowling's book, *You Mean I Don't Have to Feel This Way?* would help you become familiar with the signs of depression, and your physician or a therapist could assist you in making an assessment.

What Erodes Love?

Some life situations and specific issues erode love. Of particular note is the external pressures that homosexual relationships encounter, together with the issues that women face in general. Despite the social transformations of the last thirty years, women still earn less money than men and face subtle discriminations in the workplace and society.

Dealing with lack of money, or struggling to earn enough money, can reduce optimism about life and divert a couple's focus from activities and experiences that foster loving feelings.

Discrimination inspires anger and can influence women to feel less worthy of love and good treatment. It is a challenge for any couple to maintain loving feelings while dealing with the realities of love. Discrimination in all its forms gives lesbian couples an additional layer of difficulty to navigate.

Four main points can be made about the erosion of love in a relationship. These involve distance, external pressures, recognition as a couple, and boredom.

1. Distance. People in a relationship can be in conflict, frustrated to the point of wishing the other woman was out of her life, but a sense of involvement exists between them. Love is eroded, however, when communication stops and distance is created. Nothing — not affairs, not hostility — is equal to the effect of distance. To maintain love it is essential to maintain emotional contact.

Couples avoid emotional contact because of fear. Specific fears include that of feeling strong emotion, of the partner's response, and of judgment, humiliation, rejection, and loss. It is important to remember that emotional contact may not produce what is feared, but emotional distance definitely will.

2. Too much external pressure. External pressure may come from trouble with family, job, money, or health. There is always the hope that the close, warm contact of a loving relationship will be enough to handle such pressures, but it isn't always so.

As external pressures increase, a plan is needed to protect the loving feelings in your relationship. Increasing support for you as individuals, and as a couple, is a wise remedy. Support usually comes from friends, coworkers, family, spiritual guides, and therapists. It is also useful to increase self-care techniques that you know work for you. These could include exercise, meditation, yoga, contact with nature, and hobbies.

It is normal to need support when dealing with external pressure. Accepting support and practicing self-care are signs of strength, not weakness.

3. Recognition as a valid couple. Heterosexual couples bond together in many ways — having a wedding, being parents, setting up a home — to create a sense of a relationship. The rituals and customs around engagement and marriage show society's recognition of these relationships. To establish bonding experiences, many lesbian couples are creating their own traditions and ceremonies, which are helpful in terms of validating and celebrating their relationships.

Simple experiences such as having a relative ask "How are you two doing?" or a coworker inquire "What are you and Debbie doing over the weekend?" validate the fact that the two of you are also one. It is important to be out enough to receive this recognition in daily life.

Without external recognition and support, many lesbians understandably struggle at an emotional level to accept their relationships as truly valid ones. This makes it doubly important that they turn for support to other lesbian couples, organizations, and understanding family members.

Failing to find external recognition as a valid couple and not seeing themselves as "real" in society's eyes, two women may not fight for the continuance of their relationship in the same way that a heterosexual couple would.

4. Boredom. One of the positive aspects of a lesbian relationship — similarity — may also be one source of its downfall. Relationships between women often focus on the undoubted similarity between the partners. This can be a strength, but boredom can occur when the excitement caused by differences is absent.

It is tempting to be comfortable and unchallenged, but many lesbian couples need to make sure that they have enough stimulation to vitalize their relationship, both in personal interactions and in their lives in the outer world.

Affairs

Affairs threaten the love that exists in a relationship. They are also a sign that the love between the partners is already compromised. Affairs bring pain and are always a significant occurrence in a relationship. The woman who is having the affair is often trying to communicate something by her behavior.

- I'm angry at you.
- I'm paying you back for hurting me.
- I need attention, and you don't give it to me.
- You had an affair, and I'm evening the score.
- Our sex life isn't working.
- I'm lonely.
- I want to end our relationship but lack the courage to say this, so I'll provoke you into ending it.

Communicating directly and verbally about deep emotion can be frightening. It is rarely as devastating as communicating by means of an affair.

Some affairs happen because, regardless of what a woman says to her partner, she really does not believe in monogamy and does not practice it. When starting a relationship it is important not to assume that you share a common belief about monogamy but to discuss the subject frankly. It takes time to know someone well enough to know a person's values and whether or not she lives by what she says.

However catastrophic affairs can be, there are some couples who look back at affairs occurring during their relationship as events that led to useful learning, deepening of commitment, and greater understanding of each other.

A woman who has had an affair and wants to use the affair as an opportunity for growth needs to be willing to confront several issues:

- Her commitment to monogamy
- Her willingness to give up the pleasures of immediate gratification and understand the deeper feelings she is experiencing
- Her interest in exploring any hurt, anger, or resentment she has toward her partner
- The function sexual behavior has had in her life

Individual sexual behavior is an expression of many things. Some women are sexual to validate themselves as attractive or important. Some use sexual contact outside a relationship to create distance with a partner because they are afraid of intimacy. Some lack self-worth and are unable to say no. Some have sex because they feel degraded and continue the degradation. Some are sexually promiscuous because they crave love they did not receive as children or because they experienced sexual molestation as children, which they may or may not remember.

A woman whose partner has had an affair needs to check herself to see if she stays emotionally and sexually involved with her partner. She must make sure that conflict is dealt with until it is resolved. This does not mean that she is responsible for the affair. Rather, a relationship is a dynamic experience in which one person's feelings and behaviors affect the feelings and behavior of the other.

If a couple is dealing with an affair and wants to remain together, each must talk openly and emotionally about the pain that has resulted and, either alone or with a couples therapist, work to decode the meaning of the affair in the relationship. One or both people might seek individual counseling in order to sort out her contribution to the problem.

If a difference in values about monogamy is uncovered, it would be unwise to maintain the relationship. Personal values that are different in this area create ongoing pain, fighting, and depression.

If a self-esteem or communication problem is discovered, the affair could be the impetus needed to do emotional work that will lead to a better relationship.

Can This Relationship Be Saved?

Women caught in relationships that they know are not working properly may feel frightened and overwhelmed about facing the fact and doing something about it. Having a plan of what to do can reduce fear and give you some sense of control in your relationship, even during rocky times. Four steps can improve your relationship.

Step 1: Acknowledge the relationship is damaged. As a first step, it is crucial for both women to acknowledge that the relationship is damaged. People sometimes limp along for months, or even years, in a relationship that just isn't working. Women, being socialized to accommodate, will often endure an unrewarding relationship without openly questioning the situation.

It is necessary to be direct. "This isn't feeling good" or "My needs aren't being met" or "We're not having sex" or "This just isn't working."

Having the courage to speak out often leads to an immediate release of tension, because both women have been thinking that something is wrong but neither was willing to say it out loud. This is usually followed by feelings of regret and fear: "Are we going to break up?" or "Will we lose what is good?" or "Would it have been better not to say anything?"

Step 2: List what you need. The next step is to list what you need in an honest, nonblaming way: "I need you to spend more time with me" or "I need you to talk with me more" or "I want to make love more often/in new ways" or "We need more money/ new friends" or "I need time away from you."

Step 3: Make suggestions. Each woman must come up with suggestions about what might help. Listen carefully and share opinions about possible solutions. This is not a time to accommodate, but rather to communicate as clearly as possible.

Step 4: Try out and evaluate. This is a period of trying out and then evaluating solutions. For example, money problems may be addressed by a change of job, or by one woman taking part-time work. Too little lovemaking might mean setting aside Tuesday night to make love. Lack of social contacts could be solved by joining a softball team or by contacting friends you haven't seen for a while.

If the couple find they are unable to communicate clearly or that solutions cannot be found, they need the help of friends and family and possibly the help of professional counselors.

Practice the four steps on minor difficulties before tackling issues that bring up strong emotions. Make the four steps a part of your daily problem-solving efforts.

Why Do Couples Break Up?

There are several common reasons why women end their relationships.

Insufficient research. In the excitement of the first attraction, insufficient research is made before making a commitment. It takes three months to a year to get to know someone really well. As the realities become clear, one or other the partners may not want to continue the relationship.

Getting involved too soon. Getting involved too soon, in the early stages of a breakup of another relationship, is more than unwise. The new relationship comes into being to cushion the pain of loss. As grief subsides, the purpose of the relationship is completed.

Destructive qualities. Some of the qualities in a relationship that will weaken and often destroy it are anger, criticism, defensiveness, contempt, and stonewalling. Those five qualities are destructive to closeness and loving feelings, and often presage a breakup.

Differences are too great. Some differences, such as disagreements in values or life goals, are an impediment to a successful relationship. Most other differences present an opportunity to expand one's own life experiences and to gain the benefits of another point of view.

At first a woman may feel stimulated by a partner who is different from herself. Over time, however, the challenges in communication, problem-solving, and understanding may feel too great or too frustrating, and a breakup occurs.

Reenactment of a painful childhood experience. One or both women may have selected a partner who has personality traits or styles of interaction similar to family members who caused pain to the person when she was a child.

Pressures are too great. The couple have more pressure upon them than can be balanced by their support for each other and the support from others. Pressures can include discrimination and nonacceptance by society and family, financial and health difficulties, legal issues, deaths, problems with children.

Midlife crisis. The emotional realization that life is half over, that successes have limits, that some potential experiences are not going to happen, and that menopause is beginning can induce emotional turmoil. It is at this time that change may be embraced as a solution to the crisis, although the issue is really midlife — not the relationship.

Expressions of anger. The way in which anger

is expressed can erode loving feelings. Anger released in physical violence or verbal attacks can wound deeply and frighten. These are assaults and need to be acknowledged as such, and a commitment made to change, accompanied by a realistic plan to accomplish this change.

Unreleased anger leads to coldness and distance in a relationship and ultimately makes the other woman feel alone. She is likely to conclude she might just as well *be* alone.

Anger needs to be stated honestly and directly, with respect for, and sensitivity to, a partner. Anything else can eventually destroy a relationship.

Failure to seek guidance at a time of crisis. A crisis is an opportunity to learn, to evaluate, to move forward. Many personal and relationship crises require information or expertise that you do not readily have in hand.

If you are uncomfortable with asking for or receiving help or if you are ashamed to let people know you are experiencing a crisis, you are putting your relationship in jeopardy. At times all individuals and couples face trying situations that are beyond their experience. Appropriate guidance can make the difference between a painful loss and a time of mutual learning.

Immaturity. If a relationship is going to progress beyond dating, the ability to meet adult expectations is required. These include having one's own life, handling responsibilities, being able to share and handle frustration, being able to empathize with a partner's struggles, having the ability to be flexible, and having some ability to handle a crisis situation.

Loving feelings wither in the presence of immaturity. They cannot be sustained when life presents anything that is difficult or challenging.

Inability to love. Some women have been damaged to the degree that they are incapable of feeling warmth, caring, or love — or they have limited capacity for these feelings. In getting to know a woman like this, you would observe that she is not loving in her words, her tone, or her behavior. She doesn't have caring responses to her family or her work associates and has no warm friendships.

It is a mistake to assume that this woman just hasn't learned to open up. For some people this is a condition that persists — it is the way they are, and you cannot change them.

Attempting a relationship with a sociopath/ psychopath. Some people are completely incapable of normal human feelings. Life and relationships are a game, and they play to win. These people will do anything, say anything, to achieve personal satisfaction. Though skilled at giving the appearance of honesty and caring, these con artists exploit, not relate.

If you are hearing everything you ever wanted to hear from someone without roots, you are not in a relationship. You've become a pawn in her game.

How Do People Break Up?

There are ways that people break up that add pain to an already difficult situation. A common characteristic of these styles of ending is a lack of awareness or a lack of direct honesty.

- "I'm already gone, but I feel too guilty to leave." The person has a new love interest but denies it for a period of time. She tells her lover that she wants to leave but when the lover reacts with pain, she agrees to try to make things better. She continues contact with her new love, and ultimately breaks up with the original partner.

- "I've done the breakup in my mind, but I want to be a good person in your eyes, so I'll act like I'm trying. And then I'll leave." She withdraws over a period of time. She thinks a lot about breaking up but doesn't tell her partner the things that are wrong. There is no opportunity to work on the problems. When confronted she is likely to say, "I'm working on the relationship."

- "I want out, but I don't want the responsibility for the breakup." She provokes the partner into leaving by behaving in a way that she knows is intolerable — affairs, use of drugs or alcohol, misuse of money, or something else she knows will be unacceptable.

- "There are things about you I don't like. I'd rather leave than work toward a realistic relationship that would include things I like and things I don't."

Certainly if a woman has deliberately hidden from her lover information that has serious implications for their relationship, discovering the secret could provide the impetus to break up.

In less dramatic examples, a woman may be immature and unwilling to accept both the wonderful and the difficult aspects of her partner, or she may be someone who is searching for a perfect partner to meet her unfulfilled childhood needs. Such a woman will focus on the things she doesn't like in her partner until her negative feelings increase. She then uses anger as the stimulus to end the relationship.

- "We never argue." There are several effective methods of resolving conflict, but avoidance is not one of them. The partners who never argue likely deny to themselves that they have complaints about the relationship. If they recognize that they have complaints, they are unwilling or unable to discuss them. Such a couple breaks up with months or years of stored angers and resentments, often when one of them experiences an attraction to another woman, which, of course, feels to her temporarily fresh and resentment-free.

Danger Signs to Watch Out For

Observing the following danger signs will alert you to potential areas where your relationship may have problems.

- One person is growing and the other isn't (growth comes from such things as challenging work, 12-step programs, therapy, school, friends, special interests)

- There is no adequate support group
- No glue — that is, nothing in common,
  such as doing things together or sharing
  experiences
- Untreated personal problems such as
  depression or drug or alcohol dependence
- Secrets
- Excessive outside problems — financial, loss
  of job, moving, illness, and changes within
  the family such as deaths, divorces.

A relationship in danger is not a doomed relationship. Distancing and conflict can be signals to communicate. Through communication, love is grounded and intensifies.

Couples who regret their breakup sometimes look back and say, "I saw the signals, but I ignored them." Face the danger signs courageously, and your relationship may grow.

Chapter 12:

The Loving Lesbian

Your ability to love depends on your level of development as a person and as a woman. The more sense you have of your own inner power, the less need you will have to exploit others, to use them to fill you up, and the less likely you are to desperately hold on to whom and what you have.

Loving is a giving of yourself. It is self-expression, not draining of self. Loving is not self-sacrifice. In loving a woman, you will feel most alive and most in touch with your power.

In a loving relationship each woman overcomes a basic universal sense of isolation, yet retains her essential self.

Loving is characterized by an active concern for one's partner, with an ability and readiness to respond to her needs and feelings.

Love is a response to a known person. None of us can love in a real way without knowledge of our beloved. Knowledge of her is an ongoing quest — not to control her, but to experience her.

If we simply love, our knowledge comes from observation without any attempt to change what we see, without judgment or concern about getting our own needs met. It is as if you are carrying a camera and at a given moment you click the shutter and appreciate the photograph as it is, without posing, special lighting, cropping of the image. You feel no disappointment, only an openness to and appreciation for what the camera caught at the moment.

The ability to see a partner as she is includes letting her grow and come into consciousness in her own time and in her own way without interference.

Being *lovable* is sometimes confused with being *pleasing*. Being lovable is being open, genuine, and responsible. Pleasing is not loving. What inspires your deepest responses to a lover is her letting you see inside. The sense of her trust and vulnerability touches your heart.

If what is revealed is false, the loving response is meaningless. It is not safe to love someone who is irresponsible about her feelings or yours. Blaming you and transferring feelings from other relationships onto you muddies the exchange between you and makes it less possible for her to be lovable. Love needs to flow safely in a corridor between the two of you, uncluttered by feelings from the past.

The understanding necessary to be loving includes

both knowledge of the beloved and self-knowledge. As you make your inward journey you need to recognize your inner corridors of fear. Are you able to travel these corridors or do you block them? Can you take your beloved with you? Is it possible for you to at least raise a lantern and look in?

Your self-knowledge lets you see how far you have progressed toward accepting the truth that you are ultimately responsible for yourself, for your needs, for the life that you create. You have the power inside of you to move continuously toward the life experiences you choose.

Some people say, "I feel so much love for you," but fail to translate the feeling into loving behavior. We move from adolescence to adulthood by creating lives that, at least to some extent, express true feelings and beliefs. Adult loving includes loving behaviors as well as emotions.

Love is giving. Fear is withholding. There are people with great material wealth who cannot spend, share, or enjoy. Are they rich or poor? There are women with thoughts, feelings, talents, skills, energy, beliefs, and experiences that they are too afraid to share. They are afraid they will not be lovable; they are afraid their loving will be rejected. Paradoxically, their withholding creates what they are trying to prevent.

In a loving lesbian couple, both women maintain their integrity. Self-expression is not loss of self. Both women are sensitive to the feelings of the other. The unfolding of a woman over time allows you to know when in the day or week it's easiest for her to hear you, to know what are the words, topics, memories that stimulate her defensiveness, to know how her

menstrual cycle affects her reactivity, to know
whether humor helps in a serious discussion or
makes it worse.

"You are more sensitive to me than when we first
met" translates to "You know me well enough now to
be able to be sensitive."

"I was just being honest" is not an acceptable
disclaimer for insensitivity. It needs to be replaced
with "This is what I am aware of in me. I know that
what I'm going to say will have an impact on you.
Let me pick a time and select my words and tone of
voice so that my message will feel like sharing and
not the arrival of a grenade."

The melding of honesty and sensitivity creates
loving communication. Your honesty lets her know
you. Your sensitivity lets her feel your caring and
respect.

Close relationships stimulate the full range of
emotions, not just those of love and sexual excitement. Whatever emotions are close to the surface,
and eventually what is deep and possibly what has
never been touched before, rise and seek expression.
The sadness of losses, the greed from past depriva-
tion, the anxiety from past betrayals and lack of reassurance, clamor for release.

Love has been analyzed in fiction, song, film, and
in the laboratory, but it is still in the *experiencing* of
love that we gain a sense of its wonder and mystery.

And each experience of love is different. In this,
you cannot measure yourself against other people — it
is your individual journey, your individual delight.

This book has given guidance, but your experience
with each person is unique. Always have the courage
to love your own way.

Bibliography

Ackerman, Diane. *A Natural History of Love*. Vintage Books, New York, 1994.

Barbach, Lonnie. *For Yourself: The Fulfillment of Female Sexuality*. Doubleday & Co., New York, 1994.

Bass, Ellen and Laura Davis. *The Courage to Heal*. Harper & Row, New York, 1988.

Bradshaw, John. *Creating Love*. Bantam Books, New York, 1992.

Faderman, Lillian. *Odd Girls and Twilight Lovers*. Columbia University Press, New York, 1991.

Fromm, Erich. *The Art of Loving*. Harper & Row, New York, 1956.

Garnets, Linda D., and Douglas C. Kimmel, eds. *Psycho-*

logical Perspectives on Lesbian and Gay Male Experience. Columbia University Press, New York, 1993.

Johnson, Susan E. *Staying Power: Long Term Lesbian Couples.* The Naiad Press, Tallahassee, Fla., 1990.

LeVay, Simon, and Elisabeth Nonas. *City of Friends.* The MIT Press, Cambridge, Mass. 1995.

Nestle, Joan, ed. *The Persistent Desire.* Alyson Publications, Boston, 1992.

Penelope, Julia, and Susan Wolfe, eds. *Lesbian Culture.* The Crossing Press, Freedom, Calif., 1993.

Rich, Adrienne. *On Lies, Secrets, and Silence.* W.W. Norton and Company, New York, 1979.

Rosenfeld, Jo Ann. "Lesbian Health Issues," in *Women's Health in Primary Care.* Williams & Wilkins, Baltimore, 1997.

Schatz, B., and K. O'Hanlon. "Anti-Gay Discrimination in Medicine: Results of a National Survey of Lesbian, Gay and Bisexual Physicians." American Association of Physicians for Human Rights, San Francisco, 1994.

Simkin, R. J. "Unique Health Care Concerns of Lesbians." *Can J. Obstet Gynecol* (1993): 5:516–522.

Slater, Suzanne. *The Lesbian Family Life Cycle.* The Free Press, New York, 1995.

LAUREL by Isabel Miller. 128 pp. By the author of the beloved
Patience and Sarah.   ISBN 1-56280-146-5   10.95

LOVE OR MONEY by Jackie Calhoun. 240 pp. The romance of
real life.   ISBN 1-56280-147-3   10.95

SMOKE AND MIRRORS by Pat Welch. 224 pp. 5th Helen Black
Mystery.   ISBN 1-56280-143-0   10.95

DANCING IN THE DARK edited by Barbara Grier & Christine
Cassidy. 272 pp. Erotic love stories by Naiad Press authors.
                                        ISBN 1-56280-144-9   14.95

TIME AND TIME AGAIN by Catherine Ennis. 176 pp. Passionate
love affair.   ISBN 1-56280-145-7   10.95

PAXTON COURT by Diane Salvatore. 256 pp. Erotic and wickedly
funny contemporary tale about the business of learning to live
together.   ISBN 1-56280-114-7   10.95

INNER CIRCLE by Claire McNab. 208 pp. 8th Carol Ashton
Mystery.   ISBN 1-56280-135-X   10.95

LESBIAN SEX: AN ORAL HISTORY by Susan Johnson.
240 pp. Need we say more?   ISBN 1-56280-142-2   14.95

BABY, IT'S COLD by Jaye Maiman. 256 pp. 5th Robin Miller
Mystery.   ISBN 1-56280-141-4   19.95

WILD THINGS by Karin Kallmaker. 240 pp. By the undisputed
mistress of lesbian romance.   ISBN 1-56280-139-2   10.95

THE GIRL NEXT DOOR by Mindy Kaplan. 208 pp. Just what
you'd expect.   ISBN 1-56280-140-6   11.95

NOW AND THEN by Penny Hayes. 240 pp. Romance on the
westward journey.   ISBN 1-56280-121-X   11.95

HEART ON FIRE by Diana Simmonds. 176 pp. The romantic and
erotic rival of *Curious Wine.*   ISBN 1-56280-152-X   11.95

DEATH AT LAVENDER BAY by Lauren Wright Douglas. 208 pp.
1st Allison O'Neil Mystery.   ISBN 1-56280-085-X   11.95

YES I SAID YES I WILL by Judith McDaniel. 272 pp. Hot
romance by famous author.   ISBN 1-56280-138-4   11.95

FORBIDDEN FIRES by Margaret C. Anderson. Edited by Mathilda
Hills. 176 pp. Famous author's "unpublished" Lesbian romance.
                                        ISBN 1-56280-123-6   21.95

SIDE TRACKS by Teresa Stores. 160 pp. Gender-bending
Lesbians on the road.   ISBN 1-56280-122-8   10.95

HOODED MURDER by Annette Van Dyke. 176 pp. 1st Jessie
Batelle Mystery.   ISBN 1-56280-134-1   10.95

WILDWOOD FLOWERS by Julia Watts. 208 pp. Hilarious and
heart-warming tale of true love.   ISBN 1-56280-127-9   10.95

NEVER SAY NEVER by Linda Hill. 224 pp. Rule #1: Never get involved
with . . .   ISBN 1-56280-126-0   10.95

THE SEARCH by Melanie McAllester. 240 pp. Exciting top cop
Tenny Mendoza case.   ISBN 1-56280-150-3   10.95

THE WISH LIST by Saxon Bennett. 192 pp. Romance through
the years.   ISBN 1-56280-125-2   10.95

FIRST IMPRESSIONS by Kate Calloway. 208 pp. P.I. Cassidy
James' first case.   ISBN 1-56280-133-3   10.95

OUT OF THE NIGHT by Kris Bruyer. 192 pp. Spine-tingling
thriller.   ISBN 1-56280-120-1   10.95

NORTHERN BLUE by Tracey Richardson. 224 pp. Police recruits
Miki & Miranda — passion in the line of fire. ISBN 1-56280-118-X   10.95

LOVE'S HARVEST by Peggy J. Herring. 176 pp. by the author of
Once More With Feeling.   ISBN 1-56280-117-1   10.95

THE COLOR OF WINTER by Lisa Shapiro. 208 pp. Romantic
love beyond your wildest dreams.   ISBN 1-56280-116-3   10.95

FAMILY SECRETS by Laura DeHart Young. 208 pp. Enthralling
romance and suspense.   ISBN 1-56280-119-8   10.95

INLAND PASSAGE by Jane Rule. 288 pp. Tales exploring conven-
tional & unconventional relationships.   ISBN 0-930044-56-8   10.95

DOUBLE BLUFF by Claire McNab. 208 pp. 7th Carol Ashton
Mystery.   ISBN 1-56280-096-5   10.95

BAR GIRLS by Lauran Hoffman. 176 pp. See the movie, read
the book!   ISBN 1-56280-115-5   10.95

THE FIRST TIME EVER edited by Barbara Grier & Christine
Cassidy. 272 pp. Love stories by Naiad Press authors.
                               ISBN 1-56280-086-8   14.95

MISS PETTIBONE AND MISS McGRAW by Brenda Weathers.
208 pp. A charming ghostly love story.   ISBN 1-56280-151-1   10.95

CHANGES by Jackie Calhoun. 208 pp. Involved romance and
relationships.   ISBN 1-56280-083-3   10.95

FAIR PLAY by Rose Beecham. 256 pp. 3rd Amanda Valentine
Mystery.   ISBN 1-56280-081-7   10.95

PAYBACK by Celia Cohen. 176 pp. A gripping thriller of romance,
revenge and betrayal.   ISBN 1-56280-084-1   10.95

THE BEACH AFFAIR by Barbara Johnson. 224 pp. Sizzling
summer romance/mystery/intrigue.   ISBN 1-56280-090-6   10.95

GETTING THERE by Robbi Sommers. 192 pp. Nobody does it
like Robbi!   ISBN 1-56280-099-X   10.95

FINAL CUT by Lisa Haddock. 208 pp. 2nd Carmen Ramirez
Mystery.   ISBN 1-56280-088-4   10.95

FLASHPOINT by Katherine V. Forrest. 256 pp. A Lesbian
blockbuster!   ISBN 1-56280-079-5   11.95

CLAIRE OF THE MOON by Nicole Conn. Audio Book —Read
by Marianne Hyatt.   ISBN 1-56280-113-9   16.95

FOR LOVE AND FOR LIFE: INTIMATE PORTRAITS OF
LESBIAN COUPLES by Susan Johnson. 224 pp.
                                            ISBN 1-56280-091-4   14.95

DEVOTION by Mindy Kaplan. 192 pp. See the movie — read
the book!   ISBN 1-56280-093-0   10.95

SOMEONE TO WATCH by Jaye Maiman. 272 pp. 4th Robin
Miller Mystery.   ISBN 1-56280-095-7   10.95

GREENER THAN GRASS by Jennifer Fulton. 208 pp. A young
woman — a stranger in her bed.   ISBN 1-56280-092-2   10.95

TRAVELS WITH DIANA HUNTER by Regine Sands. Erotic
lesbian romp. Audio Book (2 cassettes)   ISBN 1-56280-107-4   16.95

CABIN FEVER by Carol Schmidt. 256 pp. Sizzling suspense
and passion.   ISBN 1-56280-089-1   10.95

THERE WILL BE NO GOODBYES by Laura DeHart Young. 192
pp. Romantic love, strength, and friendship.   ISBN 1-56280-103-1   10.95

FAULTLINE by Sheila Ortiz Taylor. 144 pp. Joyous comic
lesbian novel.   ISBN 1-56280-108-2   9.95

OPEN HOUSE by Pat Welch. 176 pp. 4th Helen Black Mystery.
                                            ISBN 1-56280-102-3   10.95

ONCE MORE WITH FEELING by Peggy J. Herring. 240 pp.
Lighthearted, loving romantic adventure.   ISBN 1-56280-089-2   11.95

FOREVER by Evelyn Kennedy. 224 pp. Passionate romance — love
overcoming all obstacles.   ISBN 1-56280-094-9   10.95

WHISPERS by Kris Bruyer. 176 pp. Romantic ghost story
                                            ISBN 1-56280-082-5   10.95

NIGHT SONGS by Penny Mickelbury. 224 pp. 2nd Gianna Maglione
Mystery.   ISBN 1-56280-097-3   10.95

GETTING TO THE POINT by Teresa Stores. 256 pp. Classic
southern Lesbian novel.   ISBN 1-56280-100-7   10.95

PAINTED MOON by Karin Kallmaker. 224 pp. Delicious
Kallmaker romance.   ISBN 1-56280-075-2   11.95

THE MYSTERIOUS NAIAD edited by Katherine V. Forrest &
Barbara Grier. 320 pp. Love stories by Naiad Press authors.
                                            ISBN 1-56280-074-4   14.95

DAUGHTERS OF A CORAL DAWN by Katherine V. Forrest.
240 pp. Tenth Anniversary Edition.   ISBN 1-56280-104-X   11.95

BODY GUARD by Claire McNab. 208 pp. 6th Carol Ashton
Mystery.   ISBN 1-56280-073-6   11.95

CACTUS LOVE by Lee Lynch. 192 pp. Stories by the beloved
storyteller.   ISBN 1-56280-071-X   9.95

SECOND GUESS by Rose Beecham. 216 pp. 2nd Amanda Valentine
Mystery.   ISBN 1-56280-069-8   9.95

A RAGE OF MAIDENS by Lauren Wright Douglas. 240 pp. 6th Caitlin
Reece Mystery.   ISBN 1-56280-068-X   10.95

TRIPLE EXPOSURE by Jackie Calhoun. 224 pp. Romantic drama
involving many characters.   ISBN 1-56280-067-1   10.95

UP, UP AND AWAY by Catherine Ennis. 192 pp. Delightful
romance.   ISBN 1-56280-065-5   11.95

PERSONAL ADS by Robbi Sommers. 176 pp. Sizzling short
stories.   ISBN 1-56280-059-0   11.95

CROSSWORDS by Penny Sumner. 256 pp. 2nd Victoria Cross
Mystery.   ISBN 1-56280-064-7   9.95

SWEET CHERRY WINE by Carol Schmidt. 224 pp. A novel of
suspense.   ISBN 1-56280-063-9   9.95

CERTAIN SMILES by Dorothy Tell. 160 pp. Erotic short stories.
                                          ISBN 1-56280-066-3   9.95

EDITED OUT by Lisa Haddock. 224 pp. 1st Carmen Ramirez
Mystery.   ISBN 1-56280-077-9   9.95

WEDNESDAY NIGHTS by Camarin Grae. 288 pp. Sexy
adventure.   ISBN 1-56280-060-4   10.95

SMOKEY O by Celia Cohen. 176 pp. Relationships on the
playing field.   ISBN 1-56280-057-4   9.95

KATHLEEN O'DONALD by Penny Hayes. 256 pp. Rose and
Kathleen find each other and employment in 1909 NYC.
                                          ISBN 1-56280-070-1   9.95

STAYING HOME by Elisabeth Nonas. 256 pp. Molly and Alix
want a baby . . . or do they?   ISBN 1-56280-076-0   10.95

TRUE LOVE by Jennifer Fulton. 240 pp. Six lesbians searching
for love in all the "right" places.   ISBN 1-56280-035-3   10.95

KEEPING SECRETS by Penny Mickelbury. 208 pp. 1st Gianna
Maglione Mystery.   ISBN 1-56280-052-3   9.95

THE ROMANTIC NAIAD edited by Katherine V. Forrest &
Barbara Grier. 336 pp. Love stories by Naiad Press authors.
                                          ISBN 1-56280-054-X   14.95

UNDER MY SKIN by Jaye Maiman. 336 pp. 3rd Robin Miller
Mystery.   ISBN 1-56280-049-3.   10.95

CAR POOL by Karin Kallmaker. 272pp. Lesbians on wheels
and then some!   ISBN 1-56280-048-5   10.95

NOT TELLING MOTHER: STORIES FROM A LIFE by Diane
Salvatore. 176 pp. Her 3rd novel.   ISBN 1-56280-044-2   9.95

GOBLIN MARKET by Lauren Wright Douglas. 240pp. 5th Caitlin
Reece Mystery.   ISBN 1-56280-047-7   10.95

LONG GOODBYES by Nikki Baker. 256 pp. 3rd Virginia Kelly
Mystery.   ISBN 1-56280-042-6   9.95

FRIENDS AND LOVERS by Jackie Calhoun. 224 pp. Mid-
western Lesbian lives and loves.   ISBN 1-56280-041-8   11.95

THE CAT CAME BACK by Hilary Mullins. 208 pp. Highly
praised Lesbian novel.   ISBN 1-56280-040-X   9.95

BEHIND CLOSED DOORS by Robbi Sommers. 192 pp. Hot,
erotic short stories.   ISBN 1-56280-039-6   11.95

CLAIRE OF THE MOON by Nicole Conn. 192 pp. See the
movie — read the book!   ISBN 1-56280-038-8   10.95

SILENT HEART by Claire McNab. 192 pp. Exotic Lesbian
romance.   ISBN 1-56280-036-1   11.95

THE SPY IN QUESTION by Amanda Kyle Williams. 256 pp.
4th Madison McGuire Mystery.   ISBN 1-56280-037-X   9.95

SAVING GRACE by Jennifer Fulton. 240 pp. Adventure and
romantic entanglement.   ISBN 1-56280-051-5   10.95

CURIOUS WINE by Katherine V. Forrest. 176 pp. Tenth Anniversary Edition. The most popular contemporary Lesbian love story.
                                        ISBN 1-56280-053-1   11.95
       Audio Book (2 cassettes)   ISBN 1-56280-105-8   16.95

CHAUTAUQUA by Catherine Ennis. 192 pp. Exciting, romantic
adventure.   ISBN 1-56280-032-9   9.95

A PROPER BURIAL by Pat Welch. 192 pp. 3rd Helen Black
Mystery.   ISBN 1-56280-033-7   9.95

SILVERLAKE HEAT: A Novel of Suspense by Carol Schmidt.
240 pp. Rhonda is as hot as Laney's dreams.   ISBN 1-56280-031-0   9.95

LOVE, ZENA BETH by Diane Salvatore. 224 pp. The most talked
about lesbian novel of the nineties!   ISBN 1-56280-030-2   10.95

A DOORYARD FULL OF FLOWERS by Isabel Miller. 160 pp.
Stories incl. 2 sequels to *Patience and Sarah.*   ISBN 1-56280-029-9   9.95

MURDER BY TRADITION by Katherine V. Forrest. 288 pp. 4th
Kate Delafield Mystery.   ISBN 1-56280-002-7   11.95

THE EROTIC NAIAD edited by Katherine V. Forrest & Barbara
Grier. 224 pp. Love stories by Naiad Press authors.
                                        ISBN 1-56280-026-4   14.95

DEAD CERTAIN by Claire McNab. 224 pp. 5th Carol Ashton
Mystery.   ISBN 1-56280-027-2   10.95

CRAZY FOR LOVING by Jaye Maiman. 320 pp. 2nd Robin Miller
Mystery.   ISBN 1-56280-025-6   10.95

STONEHURST by Barbara Johnson. 176 pp. Passionate regency
romance.   ISBN 1-56280-024-8   9.95

INTRODUCING AMANDA VALENTINE by Rose Beecham.
256 pp. 1st Amanda Valentine Mystery.   ISBN 1-56280-021-3   10.95

UNCERTAIN COMPANIONS by Robbi Sommers. 204 pp.
Steamy, erotic novel.   ISBN 1-56280-017-5   11.95

A TIGER'S HEART by Lauren W. Douglas. 240 pp. 4th Caitlin
Reece Mystery.   ISBN 1-56280-018-3   9.95

PAPERBACK ROMANCE by Karin Kallmaker. 256 pp. A
delicious romance.   ISBN 1-56280-019-1   10.95

THE LAVENDER HOUSE MURDER by Nikki Baker. 224 pp.
2nd Virginia Kelly Mystery.   ISBN 1-56280-012-4   9.95

PASSION BAY by Jennifer Fulton. 224 pp. Passionate romance,
virgin beaches, tropical skies.   ISBN 1-56280-028-0   10.95

STICKS AND STONES by Jackie Calhoun. 208 pp. Contemporary
lesbian lives and loves.   ISBN 1-56280-020-5   9.95
Audio Book (2 cassettes)   ISBN 1-56280-106-6   16.95

UNDER THE SOUTHERN CROSS by Claire McNab. 192 pp.
Romantic nights Down Under.   ISBN 1-56280-011-6   11.95

GRASSY FLATS by Penny Hayes. 256 pp. Lesbian romance in
the '30s.   ISBN 1-56280-010-8   9.95

A SINGULAR SPY by Amanda K. Williams. 192 pp. 3rd
Madison McGuire Mystery.   ISBN 1-56280-008-6   8.95

THE END OF APRIL by Penny Sumner. 240 pp. 1st Victoria
Cross Mystery.   ISBN 1-56280-007-8   8.95

KISS AND TELL by Robbi Sommers. 192 pp. Scorching stories
by the author of *Pleasures*.   ISBN 1-56280-005-1   11.95

STILL WATERS by Pat Welch. 208 pp. 2nd Helen Black Mystery.
                                            ISBN 0-941483-97-5   9.95

TO LOVE AGAIN by Evelyn Kennedy. 208 pp. Wildly romantic
love story.   ISBN 0-941483-85-1   11.95

IN THE GAME by Nikki Baker. 192 pp. 1st Virginia Kelly
Mystery.   ISBN 1-56280-004-3   9.95

STRANDED by Camarin Grae. 320 pp. Entertaining, riveting
adventure.   ISBN 0-941483-99-1   9.95

THE DAUGHTERS OF ARTEMIS by Lauren Wright Douglas.
240 pp. 3rd Caitlin Reece Mystery.   ISBN 0-941483-95-9   9.95

CLEARWATER by Catherine Ennis. 176 pp. Romantic secrets
of a small Louisiana town.   ISBN 0-941483-65-7   8.95

THE HALLELUJAH MURDERS by Dorothy Tell. 176 pp. 2nd
Poppy Dillworth Mystery.   ISBN 0-941483-88-6   8.95

SECOND CHANCE by Jackie Calhoun. 256 pp. Contemporary
Lesbian lives and loves.   ISBN 0-941483-93-2   9.95

BENEDICTION by Diane Salvatore. 272 pp. Striking, contem-
porary romantic novel.   ISBN 0-941483-90-8   11.95

TOUCHWOOD by Karin Kallmaker. 240 pp. Loving, May/
December romance.   ISBN 0-941483-76-2   11.95

COP OUT by Claire McNab. 208 pp. 4th Carol Ashton Mystery.
                                                  ISBN 0-941483-84-3   10.95

THE BEVERLY MALIBU by Katherine V. Forrest. 288 pp. 3rd
Kate Delafield Mystery.   ISBN 0-941483-48-7   11.95

THE PROVIDENCE FILE by Amanda Kyle Williams. 256 pp.
2nd Madison McGuire Mystery.   ISBN 0-941483-92-4   8.95

I LEFT MY HEART by Jaye Maiman. 320 pp. 1st Robin Miller
Mystery.   ISBN 0-941483-72-X   10.95

THE PRICE OF SALT by Patricia Highsmith (writing as Claire
Morgan). 288 pp. Classic lesbian novel, first issued in 1952 . . .
acknowledged by its author under her own, very famous, name.
                                                  ISBN 1-56280-003-5   10.95

SIDE BY SIDE by Isabel Miller. 256 pp. From beloved author of
Patience and Sarah.   ISBN 0-941483-77-0   10.95

STAYING POWER: LONG TERM LESBIAN COUPLES by
Susan E. Johnson. 352 pp. Joys of coupledom. ISBN 0-941-483-75-4   14.95

SLICK by Camarin Grae. 304 pp. Exotic, erotic adventure.
                                                  ISBN 0-941483-74-6   9.95

NINTH LIFE by Lauren Wright Douglas. 256 pp. 2nd Caitlin
Reece Mystery.   ISBN 0-941483-50-9   9.95

PLAYERS by Robbi Sommers. 192 pp. Sizzling, erotic novel.
                                                  ISBN 0-941483-73-8   9.95

MURDER AT RED ROOK RANCH by Dorothy Tell. 224 pp.
1st Poppy Dillworth Mystery.   ISBN 0-941483-80-0   8.95

A ROOM FULL OF WOMEN by Elisabeth Nonas. 256 pp.
Contemporary Lesbian lives.   ISBN 0-941483-69-X   9.95

THEME FOR DIVERSE INSTRUMENTS by Jane Rule. 208 pp.
Powerful romantic lesbian stories.   ISBN 0-941483-63-0   8.95

These are just a few of the many Naiad Press titles — we are the oldest and
largest lesbian/feminist publishing company in the world. We also offer an
enormous selection of lesbian video products. Please request a complete
catalog. We offer personal service; we encourage and welcome direct mail
orders from individuals who have limited access to bookstores carrying our
publications.